# SIMPLIFY VEGETABLE GARDENING

# SIMPLIFY VEGETABLE GARDENING

ALL THE BOTANICAL KNOW-HOW YOU NEED
TO GROW MORE FOOD AND HEALTHIER
EDIBLE PLANTS

## TONY O'NEILL

COOL
SPRINGS
PRESS

**Quarto.com**
© 2024 Quarto Publishing Group USA Inc.
Text © 2024 Tony O'Neill

First Published in 2024 by Cool Springs Press, an imprint of The Quarto Group,
100 Cummings Center, Suite 265-D, Beverly, MA 01915, USA.
T (978) 282-9590 F (978) 283-2742

Cool Springs Press titles are also available at discount for retail, wholesale, promotional, and bulk purchase. For details, contact the Special Sales Manager by email at specialsales@quarto.com or by mail at The Quarto Group, Attn: Special Sales Manager, 100 Cummings Center, Suite 265-D, Beverly, MA 01915, USA.

28 27 26 25 24          1 2 3 4 5

ISBN: 978-0-7603-8497-8

Digital edition published in 2024
eISBN: 978-0-7603-8498-5

Library of Congress Cataloging-in-Publication Data available.

Design: Emily Austin, The Sly Studio

Illustration: Ada Grave Keesler

All photos by Tony O'Neill, except for the following:

Shutterstock: pages 23 (right), 24, 25 (top), 26, 27, 29, 45, 47, 49-51, 54 (top), 65, 70, 72, 74, 77 (right), 79, 80, 85, 88 (right), 93, 95 (bottom), 100, 101 (top), 113, 121, 133 (bottom), 142, 154, 155, 158, 164 (bottom)

JLY Gardens: pages 12, 13, 14, 18, 23 (left), 44, 54 (bottom), 55, 58, 82 (top), 105, 107, 109, 110, 161, 162, 173

Alamy: page 163

Printed in China

# Dedication

To my grandfather, Ted.

The seed you planted in me all those years ago in the steep terraced allotment of Carnetown, Abercynon, has grown into a mighty oak. I was just seven
years old when you introduced me to the world of gardening, a world that
seemed daunting and thorny, much like the gooseberry bushes I would brave
for those sweet, ripe berries. I didn't realize it then, but you taught me much
more than how to tend a garden. You were teaching me about life, about
perseverance, and about love.

I remember the damp, musty smell of the old shed, covered in tin sheeting
to protect it from the weather, and your voice, firm and instructive, guiding
me through each task. "Weed here," "dig there," you would say, and I would
obey, not knowing that with each instruction, you were sowing a different kind
of seed in me. A seed that would grow into a lifelong passion for gardening
and a desire to pass on that love to my own children.

You left us when I was still in my early teens, but your legacy lives on in the
garden, in this book, and in the lessons I now share with my own children and
with people all over the world through my online content. Together, we reap
what you sowed, and not just my family but everyone who has benefited from
my content has you to thank for it.

I miss those simpler times when you were there to guide me, but I am grateful
for the wisdom you imparted and the love of gardening you instilled in me. I
miss you, Gramp. Thank you for being such an inspiration to me throughout
my life. Your love of gardening has blossomed in me, and I am forever grateful.

With all my love,

# Contents

[left] A mouthwatering truss of ripening cherry tomatoes, hanging gracefully within the Simplify Gardening tunnel, highlighting the dedication and skill required to produce such vibrant, homegrown fruits.

# Introduction

Welcome to a simplified guide to greater gardening. I'm Tony O'Neill of Simplify Gardening, and this book is dedicated to the millions of current and prospective vegetable gardeners everywhere. An early disclaimer: I am not a scientist or botanist; I am merely a firefighter impassioned by nature's wonders. I get really excited by nature's response to our efforts, the intricacies of nature's interrelated activities, and the science behind it all. I also get frustrated by humanity's lack of respect for that which sustains us.

If these things excite you too, then you'll enjoy this book. In it, we explore the growing importance of vegetables in the Anthropocene—the current, human-centric geological age—along with sixteen core strategies for successful vegetable gardening and the sixteen plant families the world relies on for food. Gardening is a fabulous endeavor that requires all our intellectual, creative, practical, and spiritual faculties—our whole being. This book is a summary of my four decades of gardening learning. Enjoy!

[top left] The thriving gardens at Simplify Gardening. Dedication to sustainable cultivation and can preserve plant varieties for future growth.

[bottom left] These bags of potting soil are stacked next to a large mound of homemade compost at the Simplify Gardening garden, highlighting the essential ingredients for a flourishing garden.

## RELATING TO NATURE

The soil scientists will say it starts in the soil—healthy soil, healthy food, healthy people.

The chemists will focus on providing a plant with its seventeen essential elements, which even allow us to grow plants in flowing water. Microbiologists will argue for the role of biodiversity in growing healthy food. All of them are right, but for me, it all starts with the gardener's relationship with nature.

A healthy relationship can be defined as one where both parties are appropriately aware of and responsive to each other's needs, which brings us to personal agency. The universal principle is to love others and control yourself, not the other way around.

Nature's response to us is at its discretion; our responsibility in the relationship is our behavior toward nature's needs. The challenge is in differentiating accurately between apparent and underlying needs. For example, plants wilt for several reasons other than insufficient water, including overwatering. Your response is a guess unless you know your plant and its environment. Gardening requires a higher level of intimacy with nature.

As a matter of urgency, we all need to develop a healthier relationship with nature. There needs to be a greater awareness of nature's needs, and that awareness should be matched by appropriate responses. Our current behavior is destroying a relationship we can't live without. Peoples' lack of appreciation for nature's limits to abuse has already triggered several tipping points, hindering what nature does best: support life.

Nature can survive without us—it would be like leaving a toxic relationship. But we can't survive without nature. We can leave the planet and go to Mars or wherever, but unless we take some of nature's genius with us, we won't survive. Nature holds the key to life. The Greek word for repentance is *metanoia* and implies changing one's way of thinking and behaving. A collective metanoia is required, starting with nature's lovers—gardeners.

## YOUR ROLE

The first third of this book focuses on your importance—gardeners and community nano-farmers. Community nano-farmers are small-scale urban farmers running commercially sustainable operations. You are humanity's hope, and the world needs hundreds of millions more like you.

Unless a significant part of each community tackles the complexities of growing food well, at scale, with limited resources, and in compromised environments, society's weaker ones will suffer—especially children. While many

A captivating shot of the flourishing gardens at Simplify Gardening, showcasing an array of productive edible plants, highlighting the garden's commitment to sustainable, efficient food-growing systems.

A delightful photo capturing me, Tony Murphy, and Worzel Gummidge, a character in a British children's storybook, smiling together in a lush garden, celebrating our shared love for gardening.

seem to adopt an "I'm okay, mate!" attitude, people in an intimate relationship with nature have more empathy and an understanding of how quickly something strong can become weak and die.

My greatest concern is for our children. It is estimated that if our diets don't change to at least 50 percent vegetables, we'll need seven planet Earths to feed the ten billion population by 2050—and that is not the distant future: it's in your child's lifetime.

The EAT-*Lancet* Commission[1], cochaired by Walter Willett and Johan Rockström, brought together nineteen commissioners and eighteen coauthors from sixteen countries in various fields, including human health, agriculture, political science, and environmental sustainability. Their report and reports from the United Nations Food and Agriculture Organization (FAO)[2] all have a similar theme: Global consumption of fruits, vegetables, nuts, and legumes will have to double, and consumption of foods such as red meat and sugar will have to be reduced by more than 50 percent. A plant-dominant diet is the only way to balance human needs and nature's capacities.

It's wise to spot emerging trends, some due to necessity, and get in front of the wave for better surfing. Communities best able to grow vegetables are the most likely to thrive in the coming decade or two. You, dear lady, dear sir, are a hero in the making.

This photo highlights sustainable food-growing practices, featuring brassicas under protective netting in ground beds. Locally grown, seasonal vegetables minimize delivery mileage.

## FOOD GARDENING EXCELLENCE

The book is divided into three sections: why, how, and what. I start with the why because, in competence development, purpose precedes process; something you'll know if you've been around a two-year-old with their incessant "why?" Little children, as soon as they can query your actions, want to know why stuff happens and why they should do certain activities, and "because I'm your mother and I said so" doesn't quite compute. Also, we learn better if our motivation is emotional. The "It's essential that we solve this" learning motivator is more effective than "Let's see what Tony thinks."

## Why?

It is essential that we become food gardening gurus—ordinary people like you and me. The book's first section explores some realities regarding the unsustainability of our current food consumption patterns, nature's actual food production capacities, and the impact of a growing population. The takeaway of the section is that we need to become better at growing more nutritious food, and we need to do it NOW!

In the first section, we explore the following topics:

- The growing importance of vegetables
- Growing food insecurities
- Sustainable food systems
- Community food systems
- Community resilience development
- Sustainable food systems and technology

- The perfect trio: science, nature, and you
- Systems awareness
- Ecological systems
- Adaptive cycles
- Biomimicry
- The success factor—YOU!

## How?

Assuming you, as I do, ascribe to the notion that more of us need to grow better food better, the logical follow-up question is "how?" There are numerous books on growing your own vegetables—this is one more, but with a twist. The book thoroughly covers the basics and then goes beyond that, looking also at why things happen.

What the world needs is expertly competent food gardeners. Learning is about more than knowing something. Cognitive knowledge, without understanding, creates expert novices—people who can recite information but are not able to interrogate or explore its application in different contexts.

According to Bloom's taxonomy of learning, there are six levels to transforming basic understanding into expert competency.

- Remembering—the ability to recall information
- Understanding—the ability to rephrase, describe, provide an example, and summarize
- Applying—a transition from head knowledge to practical application

- Analyzing—the ability to compare and find relational links between know-how topics
- Evaluating—the ability to hypothesize new possibilities in applying current knowledge
- Creating—the ability to produce expanded know-how

Remembering is defined as lower-level thinking. Our aim is to move well beyond that to higher-level thinking skills. We're interested in minimally reaching a competency level beyond applied knowledge, exploring and testing alternatives.

We will focus on these sixteen core gardening strategies:

- Regenerative gardening principles—ensure you take less than nature can regenerate

- Propagating plants—increase your plant starting success rates

- Soil health—develop an optimized growing environment, even in harsh conditions

- Root health—optimize your plants' access to underground resources

- Foliar health—understand the four levels of synthesis

- Composting—reduce organic waste to essential carbon and humus

- Plant nutrition—add less, improve availability

- Organic fertilizer—work with nature's provisions

- Mulching—learn the how, when, and why of using ground covers

- Plant support—maximize yields by going vertical

- Seed saving—improve future crop resilience to local growing conditions

- Light and darkness—manipulate photoperiodism for maximum gains

- Water management—grow plants in arid, hot environments—a zero waste approach

- Temperature—understand the role of soil and ambient temperatures in plant starting and growth

- Pest management—use nature's pest management strategies and alternatives to pesticides that work

- Disease Management—avoid and manage plant diseases

[page left] Artichokes are members of the Asteraceae, one of the largest floral plant families.

[page right, left] Fava beans are a member of the Fabaceae, a family of legume plants notable for their ability to form symbiotic associations with nitrogen-fixing microorganism.

[page right, right] Pumpkins are a member of the Cucurbitaceae, a family of plants with tendril-bearing vines that also includes melons, cucumbers, squash, and gourds.

# What?

The final section of this book covers growing the eighty most common food and herb plants, grouped into sixteen plant families.

- **Amaranthaceae:** amaranth, beets, lamb's-quarters, quinoa, spinach, Swiss chard

- **Amaryllidaceae:** chives, garlic, leeks, onions, scallions, shallots

- **Apiaceae:** angelica, anise, caraway, carrot, celery, cilantro (coriander), cumin, dill, fennel, lovage, parsley, parsnip

- **Asteraceae:** artichokes, endives, lettuce, sunflowers

- **Brassicaceae:** broccoli, Brussels sprouts, cabbage, cauliflower, kale, kohlrabi, mustard, radishes, rutabaga, turnip

- **Convolvulaceae:** sweet potato

- **Cucurbitaceae:** cucumbers, gourds, melons, pumpkins, squashes (summer), squashes (winter)

- **Dioscoreaceae:** yam

- **Euphorbiaceae:** cassava

- **Fabaceae:** beans, chickpeas, fava beans, lentils, lima beans, peas, soybeans

- **Lamiaceae:** basil, hyssop, lavender, marjoram, mint, oregano, perilla, rosemary, sage, savory, thyme

- **Malvaceae:** okra

- **Musaceae:** plantain

- **Poaceae:** barley, corn, pearl millet, oats, rye, wheat

- **Polygonaceae:** rhubarb

- **Solanaceae:** eggplant, pepper (hot), pepper (sweet), potato, tomato

Finally, I want to thank you for buying the book, and I hope it will be a continued source of inspiration for years to come. I have tried summarizing what the last four decades of vegetable gardening have taught me, with science at my side. Your success at vegetable gardening is essential, and I hope this helps.

Home gardens are an important piece of the food security puzzle.

# Chapter 1:

## The Growing Importance of Vegetables

Our food system is broken. Planet Earth currently has eight billion human inhabitants, none of whom had a say in their birth, but all needing food daily. Food security is having access to enough food to sustain health and normal development. According to a U.S. Department of Agriculture (USDA) report, the number of food insecure people globally in 2022 is estimated at 1.3 billion, an increase of 118.7 million people (almost 10 percent) from the 2021 estimate.[3]

Unless you're directly affected by food insecurity, it is normal to have a myopic perspective. If you are not part of the numbers above and below, it's tempting to apportion blame. But we have no right to take the moral high ground. Agricultural productivity is subject to factors such as regional soil fertility, rainfall, access to water, climate conditions, and the general availability of farming resources. Local food production capacities are impacted by extreme weather events linked to climate change, land degradation, and biodiversity loss. A successful response to food insecurity will need to be systems-based and consider the full scope and complexity of these issues.

Food insecurity is a serious issue that affects millions of Americans. According to the USDA, food insecurity means insufficient food for an active, healthy life, and it can lead to negative health outcomes, especially for children. The COVID-19 pandemic has worsened the situation, as people lost their jobs and income. Feeding America estimates that 53 million Americans relied on food banks and community programs in 2021 to get enough food.[4]

The problem is systemic, and each change has a ripple effect through the individual systems. It is an inherent feature of systems to remain in balance, so they are averse to change.

One of the few things effective at changing a system is a crisis—and in my humble opinion, we have one. If we don't take action soon, our children will inherit a planet that has been severely degraded, with many more people suffering from malnutrition and preventable diseases.

A study[5] by the Rockefeller Foundation on the actual cost of food, considering health outcomes, health care costs, environmental costs, and social impacts, shows that the true cost is at least three times the current annual expenditure on food of US$1.1 trillion.

[top] The essence of modern farming practices, as a combine harvester efficiently gathers barley from a field and transfers the yield directly to a waiting truck for transport.

[bottom] An imposing image of a vast wheat field, symbolizing the need for innovative and sustainable agricultural practices to ensure long-term food security.

[page right] A striking photo of barren supermarket vegetable shelves, visually emphasizing the urgent need to reevaluate and improve our global food system for a more sustainable future.

## SUSTAINABLE FOOD SYSTEMS

The United Nations FAO defines a sustainable food system as one that "delivers food security and nutrition for all in such a way that the economic, social, and environmental bases to generate food security and nutrition for future generations are not compromised."[6] In other words, a sustainable food system is financially viable and sustainable, benefits everyone equally, and doesn't negatively impact nature's ability to sustain future life on the planet.

The inseparable links between food, health, and environmental sustainability must be our critical motivators in creating a comprehensively sustainable food system for the Anthropocene. The world's food system must operate within limits for human health needs and production capacities to guarantee nutritious meals from environmentally friendly sources and be able to feed nearly ten billion people by 2050.

### Planetary Boundaries

The Stockholm Resilience Centre at Stockholm University defined nine planetary boundaries within which future generations of humans can maintain their current level of prosperity. These are key risk areas that help define the limits of our planet within which we can safely operate without compromising the sustainability of future generations.

It is argued that pushing past these boundaries increases the likelihood of causing widespread, rapid, and perhaps irreversible, environmental shifts. The planetary boundaries framework[7] has become a global standard in research, policy, and solution development. The nine measurables include:

- Novel entities (non-natural substances such as plastic)
- Stratospheric ozone depletion
- Atmospheric aerosol loading
- Ocean acidification
- Biogeochemical usage (nitrogen and phosphorus)
- Freshwater use
- Changes in land-use
- Biosphere integrity
- Climate change

The EU has applied the framework in a more condensed format. We explore the framework's nine planetary risk domains in the next chapter and explain why vegetable growing is an essential feature of a more sustainable planet.

## The Planetary Diet

Food production bears significant responsibility for current environmental degradation and planetary boundary-crossing, causing escalating disastrous effects. The world's food system requires a dramatic overhaul, both in terms of what is grown and how it's cultivated. Substantial scientific evidence connects dietary choices to human health and ecological sustainability.

It is beyond the scope of this book to address all the facets and features of humanity's food consumption habits. Fascinating is the work by the EAT-*Lancet* Commission, especially their Healthy Diets from Sustainable Food Systems Summary Report.[8] The report explores two contending tensions of feeding a growing population: human nutritional needs versus Earth's sustainable production capacities. Balancing the tensions between these two systems is complex.

The report compares the diet choices and their quantified production impact on the environment, including the systemic boundaries for:

- Greenhouse gas (GHG) emissions and their impact on climate change
- Cropland use rates and their effect on the broader ecosystem
- Water use and its impact on freshwater availability
- Nitrogen applications and their impact on nitrogen cycling
- Phosphorus applications and their effect on phosphorus cycling
- Biodiversity loss—the extinction of species

A critical facet of diet is health, which ripples through the system, impacting health care systems, and causing loss of life quality. There is extensive empirical evidence that a shift to the suggested predominant plant-based diet would reduce mortality rates in adults by between 19 and 24 percent. Extensive research on the effects of different diets on the environment has emerged, with most

A shift to producing more food on smaller, more sustainable farms is one strategy for reducing agriculture's impact on our environment.

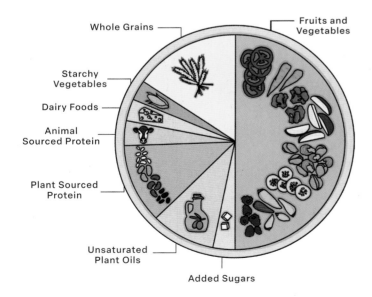

Whole Grains

Fruits and Vegetables

Starchy Vegetables

Dairy Foods

Animal Sourced Protein

Plant Sourced Protein

Unsaturated Plant Oils

Added Sugars

This is what a meal should look like in terms of a healthy balance between the food groups. Unfortunately, most meals consumed around the globe today do not follow this guideline.

studies confirming that eating more plant-based foods and less meat is better for both human health and the planet.

The report suggests five strategies for ensuring a sustainable food system:

- Shifting toward healthier, sustainable dietary habits
- Shifting agricultural priorities from quantity to nutritional quality
- Adopting food-growing methods that have a lower impact on the environment
- Not expanding the amount of land used for agriculture
- Cutting food waste levels, at least by 50 percent

## Global Shift to Healthier Diets

I'm not advocating for or against vegetarianism or veganism, but I support a change in behavior that allows our children to have a promising future. Unless we follow the advice of those who spent their lives exploring sustainable solutions, counterbalanced by a touch of skepticism for possible corporate influence, we're stuck without a departure point from which we can move toward an improved future. Minimally, our actions should prevent leaving our children with an ecosystem beyond the point of no return.

The suggested planetary health diet includes all the food groups and types, but to achieve sustainability we need to change how much of each group we collectively eat. The pie chart (left) shows the recommended splits.

Vegetable production rates would have to minimally increase by 75 percent, if not doubled. Red meat and egg production levels will have negative growth over the coming decades to limit their production environmental impact. Irrespective of how you cut the pie, the future is one where vegetable demand is high.

## The Importance of Nutritional Food

According to chairperson U.S. Senator Booker of the Subcommittee on Food and Nutrition, Specialty Crops, Organics, and Research hearing in November 2021, one in every three dollars of the U.S. federal budget goes to health care spending, with 80 percent of that spent on treating preventable diseases.[9]

The statement[10] of Dariush Mozaffarian, M.D., Dr.PH, at the hearing gives us a glimpse into the enormity of the nutritional crisis in the United States. According to him, only 6.8 percent of American adults are metabolically healthy, and health issues are predominantly dietary related. Seventy-one percent of young Americans between seventeen and twenty-four are ineligible to serve in the military due to obesity.

Malnutrition cannot be addressed without tackling issues of agriculture, health, and environmental sustainability. A holistic strategy dealing with agriculture, food, the environment, the economy, and human health needs to be developed. Current dietary choices have an enormous cost.

In addition to taking a heavy toll on people's health and longevity, the high rates of diet-related chronic diseases in the United States impose a significant financial burden on individuals, the health care system, and the economy. To ensure future generations have access to safe and secure food supplies, we must ensure that our practices across the entire food and agriculture value chain promote environmental and human health.

[top] An inviting image of a leek bed, featuring deep green foliage and mulched with chopped canola straw. It exemplifies environmentally friendly gardening practices that promote healthy plant growth.

[bottom] A proud moment captured as I hold three large, vibrant eggplants grown in my polytunnel, showcasing the fruitful results of dedicated gardening and expert cultivation.

### A Healthy Balance

Healthy eating is the practice of eating a mix of nutritious foods. Satiation and nutrition often are conflicting concepts, the former a feeling of being full and the latter ensuring health and vitality.

## The Benefits of Perennials

Perennial vegetables have higher nutritional value than annuals, and they can be harvested earlier and later in the season. Perennials improve soil health by reducing erosion, supporting beneficial microbes, and suppressing weeds. Unlike annuals, perennial vegetables don't need replanting, saving time and labor. Some examples of perennial vegetables are asparagus, rhubarb, sorrel, and Jerusalem artichoke.

A picturesque asparagus bed highlights the plant's nature as a perennial, returning each year with minimal effort. Mulching helps to conserve moisture and support healthy growth.

## Healthier Food-Growing Methods

We cover all the different gardening strategies in future chapters, including regenerative gardening. A healthier way of growing food includes switching from heavy tillage monocropping to diversity awareness in soil biota and surface plants. Several vegetables grown as annuals can be grown as perennials, and I have spinach plants that are now in their third season. The nightshade family (Solanaceae) can all be grown as perennials if they're protected from frost and freezing temperatures.

## Redefining Land-Use

In the next section, we explore the role of localized food production. The principle is to reduce mass-produced food grown in distant locations and the transportation needed to ship them.

While the planetary boundaries framework focuses on risks, mitigating these risks requires action. To do this effectively, a systems approach is essential. For example, trees are able to store underground water and retrieve it for later use, and their later transpiration affects downwind crop production levels. Everything fits together, and an action on one part impacts the whole system positively or negatively.

Often implementing these actions is challenged by conspiracy theorists and political disinformation campaigns. Fearful that the 1992 UN Agenda 21 was some disenfranchisement mechanism, objectors used community land-use committees to derail efforts at creating a more sustainable local environment.

Fear, though often irrational, is a strong motivator. In Greek mythology, Cassandra, a princess of Troy, was gifted with the ability to predict the future but cursed that she would never be believed. Although she warned of Troy's invasion and fall, she could not prevent it. This is known as the Cassandra dilemma and is ubiquitous in climate change or sustainability conversations.

While I realize we're all part of a social system that includes diverse opinions as a form of balancing power distribution, it's hard for me to see how one could deny our impact on the environment. A few come to mind:

- The impact of plastic on rivers, oceans, and landfills
- The felt impact of global warming, a product of greenhouse gas emissions
- The visible drop in air pollution levels during the COVID-19 shutdown in various cities

I'm advocating for land-use principles that provide every community with several safe spaces encouraging inclusive participation in a food system, including production, processing, distribution, consumption, and waste management (composting). I am promoting the protection of local forests, wooded areas, and water bodies. And, as the focus of this book suggests, I strongly encourage domestic vegetable gardens as an essential strategy. One that is, ideally, incentivized.

## Food Waste

Food waste has a financial and environmental impact, and according to some estimates, is responsible for 6 percent of global greenhouse gas emissions (higher than the airline industry). Discarded food wastes food, and it also wastes all the resources that went into its production, processing, transportation, preparation, and storage.

Because of its large footprint in terms of greenhouse gases (GHG), food waste contributes significantly to the global warming crisis, releasing massive amounts of carbon dioxide ($CO_2$) during food production, transport, and handling. Then, when it ends up in landfills, decomposing food produces methane, an even more potent greenhouse gas. Reducing food waste can help save money, conserve resources, and protect the environment.

The U.S. Environmental Protection Agency (EPA) 2021 report[11] on the environmental effects of food waste is shocking. EPA estimates that food waste in the United States annually accounts for 170 million $MTCO_2e$ GHG emissions, equal to the $CO_2$ emissions forty-two coal-fired power plants would produce. According to EPA statistics, 24 percent of landfill waste and 22 percent of municipal solid waste incinerated in the United States is wasted food. The report also emphasizes the savings in arable land, freshwater, fertilizer, and energy that can result from reducing food loss and waste.

In addition to mitigating the effects of climate change on the supply chain, reducing food waste can boost food security, productivity, and economic efficiency, and it can encourage resource and energy conservation. Wasting food in a world with so much hunger and malnutrition makes no sense. Much of the waste is caused by systemic failures, such as breaks in the cold chain and inter-border delays. An effective food system optimizes the balance between food production, consumption, and impacts on environmental resources. Food distribution is made easier by food drying, freezing, or canning, but these life-extension strategies impact nutritional value. Decentralized food production, such as localized vegetable gardens, can help reduce food wastage and improve the community's food system.

A powerful image depicting discarded food, illustrating the harsh reality that one-third of all food produced globally is wasted, urging us to reevaluate our consumption habits and strive for a more sustainable future.

## COMMUNITY FOOD SYSTEMS

This section explores our food systems and considers alternatives that will improve local resilience, boost local economies, and strengthen social fiber.

### Conventional Food System

Food choices are shaped by food systems, and in the United States, less than twenty giant multinational corporations produce what's available on store shelves.[12] These large-scale, product-specific companies also have stakes in farming input commodities (e.g., seed and fertilizer), marketing, processing, distribution, wholesale, and retail outlets. The most affected food sectors include meat processing, dairy products, grain processing, groceries, and food processors. The least affected are fresh produce, though farmers often are contracted to supply chain stores at cutthroat prices.

To survive, producers must maintain low per-unit costs and compete with corporates with a monopoly on processing and distribution channels. To benefit from the scale of these capacities, farmers generally opt to be contractually bound to supply these larger organizations. The shortsighted practice of forward selling forces farmers into perpetual cycles of debt and contractual obligations, leaving them with limited negotiation options. In the last few decades, most processing plants have been relocated to major production areas, leaving some regions with no local processing options. Small- to medium-size farms have essentially been elbowed out.

### Growing Local Vegetables

If food choices are influenced by food systems, then communities must have some control of the local food-story narrative. I've also noted that irrespective of how you divide the dietary plate, vegetables (should) dominate. In addition to climate change challenges, communities must navigate declining economies, health issues, lack of comprehensive inclusion, and stresses that often consume most of our available frontal cortex bandwidth.

A given, though, is that we all have to eat, generally daily. For our own health, that eating has to be considerate and thoughtful. Food is one of culture's most extensive and ingrained aspects and a distinctively human trait. Cultural norms dictate standards of food preparation and consumption. Food culture is pervasive, and frequently

A vivid image of ripe tomatoes thriving in my polytunnel at Simplify Gardening, emphasizing the importance of growing vegetables at home to reduce food miles and $CO_2$ emissions for a more sustainable lifestyle.

### Cutting Food Miles

Food miles are the distance that food travels from where it is grown to where it is consumed. Shorter food supply chains can help prevent some of the negative impacts of the global food trade, including reduced greenhouse gas emissions from transport and food waste. As a result, there is more demand for local food production to reduce food miles. Building self-determination capacities (agency) in local communities, increasing our resilience, and ring-fencing fiscal spending to local advantage are vital. Localized food production also improves product freshness, reduces food waste, and significantly reduces the added costs of storage and transport.[13][14]

cultures are defined and characterized by the food they consume. Localized food systems can better cater to the diverse specifics of cultures in a given region—both in the eating habits

Sustainable regional development strategies would do well to include local food production as one of their cornerstones. The cultural and historical ties between different regions give the people who produce the food there a sense of shared history and identity. Consumers tend to place a high value on regionally grown foods.

The most significant benefits of localizing a food system are improved financial, social, health, and ecological outcomes. The idea of local agency, the ability to retain and exercise some control, is of growing importance in a world fast becoming owned by the few at the expense of the many. In simplified terms, the strength of local economies depends on more money flowing in than on what flows out. If more money leaves a community than what comes in, it's in a perpetual state of depletion. Community food systems have the potential to boost local economies while creating a collective sense of ownership and autonomy.

[bottom left] Shopping at farmers' markets, co-ops, and CSAs is one way to shorten food supply chains and lower food miles.

[bottom right] A lively scene of people purchasing locally produced vegetables, illustrating the positive impact of community food production on fostering connections, boosting local economies, and promoting sustainability in neighborhoods.

## Scaled Local Food Systems

Urban and peri-urban agriculture is an effective strategy to address local food insecurities and develop better community resilience to disasters. Local is generally defined as produced within a 100-mile (160-km) radius, though this definition can change depending on population density. Local citizens often are willing to pay a premium for the quality benefit and the knowledge that their purchase contributes to social, environmental, and community improvements.

The collaborative and intersecting processes that connect environmentally responsible food production, processing, distribution, consumption, and waste recovery make up a community food system. Referring to our earlier definitions of food systems, the objective of community food systems is to improve the environmental, economic, social, and nutritional health of the community it serves. A functional community food system integrates all five of these subsystems.

Buying into a community food system helps safeguard the health of local economies, ensuring stakeholders can operate their stake in the system sustainably. In addition, it establishes a connection between customers and the whole food system, improving individual and community health.

In the next chapter, we explore the different factors that could contribute to the success of a community food system. These success factors often are ignored or not

directly considered, but they play a vital role in any of the community food system strategies, which can take on a variety of forms:

· Community Supported Agriculture (CSAs)

· Growers, processing, packaging, distribution, and composting cooperatives

· Farmers' markets

· Collaborations between producers, local restaurants, and chefs

· Inclusive community gardens or allotments

· Farm-to-school, -hospital, -college, and -institution programs

· U-pick operations and roadside stands

· Food banks and community food pantries

· Partnerships with local charities and community kitchens

When considered from the view of asset-based community economic development, the community food system will include most of these components and markets. However, it will also seek to build on local needs, resources, design, investment, and control to become more locally integrated and community-based. Let's explore the two leading options.

Freshly harvested vegetables being placed into wooden crates showcase the collaborative spirit and shared prosperity fostered by agricultural cooperatives, promoting sustainable and community-driven food production.

### *Agricultural Cooperatives*

A community food system consists of several components, each potentially being an interdependent business opportunity. These can be divided into separate cooperatives. Members of an agricultural cooperative benefit from working in a unified business setting. Individual farmers can save money by purchasing supplies in bulk and increasing their access to larger markets by working together. Farmers can boost productivity and income by adopting this strategy. Principles that undergird cooperative food systems include:

· Voluntary and open membership

· Democratic member control

· Members' economic participation

· Autonomy and independence

· Cross co-op cooperation

· Information, education, and training

· Serving the interests of the community

From the perspective of food gardeners, vegetable growing is a crucial function. However, growers can suffer significant losses if plant varieties, harvesting times, and quantities are not contextualized within the more extensive food system. Profitability, resource conservation, and healthy relationships are all essential components of a sustainable food production system.

Growers can decide to process their vegetables themselves or have a third-party, onsite processing unit. A better option, in my opinion, is agricultural cooperatives. According to USDA[15], agricultural cooperatives operate in more than 9,500 locations across fifty states. Some cooperatives go even further by providing health care, housing, internet and e-connectivity, and other essential services to rural areas. More than 30,000 cooperatives in the United States employ more than 2 million people, have more than 350 million members, and bring in more than US$660 billion annually.

Internet technologies can help boost cooperative efficiencies; we will explore these in the next section. Several statutory provisions[16] apply to agricultural cooperatives, making them a great trade mechanism option in community food systems. The USDA[17] also offers the

Value-Added Producer Grant (VAPG) program to help agricultural producers enter value-added activities to generate new products, create and expand marketing opportunities, and increase producer income.

Business transparency, economic opportunities, and mitigated risks are essential benefits of agricultural co-ops. These advantages prompt agricultural producers globally, with 80 percent of Argentina's agribusiness facilitated by localized cooperatives.

### Community Supported Agriculture

For farmers, the CSA is fundamentally about creating a community of patrons who are invested in their success. Before the growing season begins, customers typically purchase memberships or shares in a farm operation by sponsoring the farm's costs for the coming growing season. Customers receive products regularly throughout the growing season, most commonly a weekly vegetable box, in exchange for their financial investment. The members are all equally at risk if the farm has a bad year and output falls.

While farmers typically start CSAs, some groups have been created by customers. Community members can get together in a nontraditional setting like a CSA and work on solving pressing issues. There are CSAs with pricing structures that are designed to ensure that low-income families are not priced out of participating in the CSA program. Several CSAs are even structured as part of regional food banks, and some even create employment opportunities for at-risk groups such as the homeless.

As entrepreneurs and market forces have created new opportunities for implementing the CSA business model, the CSA model has changed significantly from its early operations. Among the current trends reshaping the CSA business are new products, extended seasons, multi-farm collaborations, new shareholder groups, collaborative marketing with various organizations, novel aggregation and delivery strategies, new connections to urban production, and health and wellness alliances.

## Small-Scale Food Systems

Home gardens are a crucial component of the regional food system. According to the National Gardening Association, 35 percent of U.S. households grew their own vegetables and fruits in 2021.[18] As well as increasing vegetable consumption (by two servings per day for gardeners compared to nongardeners), lowering food costs, and preserving family food traditions, home gardens have many other health, social, and financial advantages. Although there are many reasons people grow their own food, access to a home garden positively correlated with more servings and a wider variety of consumed fruits and vegetables.

The University of Florida has a great free resource[19] to help vegetable gardeners calculate vegetable gardening costs.

[top] Eight pairs of hands, each tenderly holding a small plant, symbolize the unity and shared commitment fostered by Community Supported Agriculture (CSAs), which empowers local farmers and encourages sustainable food practices.

[bottom] This kale is flourishing in a compact garden, highlighting the potential and benefits of growing nutrient-rich vegetables even in limited spaces, promoting self-sufficiency and sustainability.

# COMMUNITY RESILIENCE DEVELOPMENT

Resilience is the ability to bounce back from life's challenges—and we can all agree there are plenty. A product can be considered resilient if it can withstand harsh environments without failing, for example like fire truck hoses. Community resilience lies in its ability to fully recover from disasters, and these can be varied too, from hurricanes to pandemics, from droughts to floods.

What allows some communities to weather the storm better than others? Studies find that resiliency is, in part, a reflection of the diversity of community characteristics. Common features include proper planning and an inclusive "if this, then that" process, followed by effective execution of plans and policies by a broad stakeholder base. When disaster strikes, these plans and training allow community members to focus on maintaining essential functions, reducing the impact of anxiety and feeling overwhelmed.

A firefighter, like myself, is less stressed about entering a burning building than you probably are. This is because I have had the training, have done it before, and have several plans of what to do in any given situation. I am resilient to events that would traumatize others, though I'm not unaffected, just more resilient.

It all starts with the shared vision members have for the community, followed by developing a strategy for its realization. The plan should include risk management strategies and represent the aspirations and fears of all the community members.

Developing social connections might be the most crucial emergency preparedness measure. Healthy, reciprocating connections are built over time and should be a primary focus for everyone. You can never do it right in a crisis if you haven't done it right in a time of stability. Think and plan for tomorrow—for you, your family, and the greater community.

## Resilient Food Strategies

So, how do we strengthen the local food system, ensuring better food security now and in times of crisis? Here are some tips.

Gain the knowledge needed to grow your own food well. Books like this and others can help you but require you to activate what you think you know. There is no better teacher than Mother Nature, so work with her. It's like raising children; we're only fully qualified to give parenting advice once our children are healthy adults. Until then, we're all still learning.

We are stronger in groups. Work to build relationships with other gardeners and gardening communities, creating supportive networks. As we'll see later in this book, robust systems are strengthened by diversity, allowing different parts to specialize and contribute to a symbiotic whole.

A food system with many smaller interrelating gardens is more resilient to adversity than a single farm trying to do it all. Collaboration allows a community to create economies of scale, where different parts of the gardening community contribute their specialized knowledge or produce to strengthen the whole.

Food systems have long been susceptible to dangers, such as pests and severe weather, that impair the efficient operation of their numerous interdependent components. With climate-related shocks and stresses exacerbating already-present threats to food systems, now is a crucial time to assess food system vulnerabilities and take steps to mitigate them. Policymakers and academics increasingly turn to resilience to forecast, evaluate, and enhance how systems and actors respond to disruption.

Sustainability and climate change are related but distinct concepts requiring urgent action. While sustainability is concerned with addressing the needs of the present without endangering the future, climate change is concerned with preventing or adjusting to changes in the Earth's climate brought on by human activity.

### *Food Security*

Food security is a complex and multidimensional concept that aims to ensure all people have adequate access to safe and nutritious food. According to the World Bank[20], four pillars support food security, and unless all four are strong, a community is at risk.

The four pillars are:

- Availability: a sufficient local, national, and global food supply. Availability depends on factors such as food production, stock levels, trade, and distribution.

- Accessibility: people's physical and economic ability to obtain enough food for their needs. Accessibility depends on income, prices, markets, infrastructure, and social protection.

- Quality: nutritional value, safety, and diversity of food that meets people's dietary needs and preferences for an active and healthy life. Quality depends on food processing, preparation, storage, hygiene, and fortification factors.

- Stability: consistency and reliability of food availability, accessibility, and quality over time. Stability depends on weather conditions, political stability, economic shocks, and environmental degradation.

To achieve food security, communities should meet all four pillars concurrently for households or regions. If any of them is weak or disrupted, it can lead to food insecurity, which can negatively impact health, well-being, development, and peace.

[page left, left] A diverse group working harmoniously in a community garden illustrates the powerful connections and sense of belonging shared gardening experiences can foster among neighbors.

[page left, right] As older residents diligently tend a garden together, their commitment to providing fresh, homegrown food for the entire community's benefit is obvious while showcasing the timeless appeal of gardening across generations.

[right] Even small, urban, backyard gardens can improve our food system and reduce vulnerabilities.

## Hunger-Free Communities

USDA's National Institute of Food and Agriculture (NIFA)[21] has a list of actions communities can take to ensure better food security. They are:

- Having a community-based emergency food delivery network that works with programs such as food pantries, food banks, and places where people can get meals together.

- Looking at how food insecurity affects the community and what services are already there will help figure out what needs to be done to address the gaps.

- Establishing a committee that includes people with lived experience of food insecurity to evaluate current systems, explore the underlying causes, and develop policies and programs to fight food insecurity.

- Participating in nutrition programs supported by the federal government should be easy for the people they are meant to get to, such as school breakfast, school lunch, summer food, food for childcare, and food for the homeless and older people.

- Using public and private resources, including local businesses, to help people who don't have enough food.

- Having a program to teach people about the community's food needs and the need for more local people to get involved in activities to reduce food insecurity.

- Having public and private programs and services accessible through information and referral services.

- Creating creative ways to get food, such as community gardens, buying clubs, food cooperatives, grocery stores owned and run by the community, and farmers' markets, to make it easier for people to buy food.

- Doing things to find and target food services to people at high risk.

- Having good ways to get food from all sources to people who need it.

- Coordinating food services with park and recreation programs and other community outlets that are easy for people to get to.

- Getting better public transportation, services for people in need, and food.

- Having nutrition education programs for people with low incomes so they can learn how to grow, buy, and prepare food better and become more aware of the link between diet and health.

- Having a program to collect and give out healthy food that would otherwise go to waste, such as surpluses from grocers, farmers, and diners.

## SUSTAINABLE FOOD SYSTEMS AND TECHNOLOGY

According to USDA's 2021 Price Spread from Farmer to Consumer Report[22], farmers typically only get 25 percent of the prices consumers pay for their crops, with the rest spread across transportation, re-packaging, and mark-ups for the intermediaries. Localized farming and direct selling to consumers removes many costs and makes farming more profitable.

At the same time, it's important to turn our attention to minimizing input costs to further improve profitability and business sustainability. Accurately managing input variables requires a granular awareness of climate, soil, and crop conditions. At scale, this is only possible if we use emerging technologies, including sensors connected to the Internet of Things (IoT) and the scaled data processing capacities of Machine Learning (ML).

Solutions need not be expensive and can be offset if community gardens work together. In the United States, funding is available from the Office of Urban Agriculture and Innovative Production (OUAIP)[23] for similar projects. My opinion? Avoid becoming reliant on state funding. If at all possible, retain your autonomy of action and thought.

Gardeners can continue relying on their senses and experience to make decisions, but using handheld instruments to measure light levels, soil moisture, and temperatures, and connecting these to a network can vastly improve your gardening efficacy. The latest sentient devices allow insights previously only wished for, including monitoring leaf nitrogen levels and visual crop monitors able to track pollinator and pest activities.

What could offer more stability than growing and preserving some of your own food?

### Data Preprocessing

Digital technologies can help improve operational profits by improving productivity and resilience through more efficient use of resources. Relevant digital technologies include smart agriculture applications allowing precision agriculture, improved irrigation and fertilizer applications, waste management, and better risk management using AI.

Microcontrollers are scaled-down computers providing processing power, memory, and input/output peripherals. These small computers use minimal energy and can run off solar systems supported by long-lasting batteries, yet can deliver sufficient computing power for complex data processing and interconnectivity. Popular IoT board sellers are Arduino, BeagleBoard, MinnowBoard, and Raspberry Pi.

Plants with an AI overlay, showcasing the practical application of artificial intelligence in detecting and managing pest issues, contributing to healthier and more sustainable garden environments.

## Local Network or Internet Connectivity

The microprocessors are generally connected to a central hub designed to meet the transmission types, which may include ethernet cabling, Wi-Fi, Bluetooth, cellular (3G/4G/5G/LTE), NFC (Near Field Communication), LoRaWAN[24], or Swarm. Internet of Things (IoT) most commonly uses the MQ Telemetry Transport (MQTT)[25] communication protocol, which offers a small code footprint, security, reliability, and needs minimal network bandwidth.

## Data Storage and Analytics

Cloud computing can be expensive, especially if you send data to the cloud every few minutes. Ideally, you want your computing done as close to the data source as possible. Invest in local computing power to do some analyses before sending data packets to the cloud for storage. Localized ML, or ML on the edge, is now possible with the introduction of TinyML[26] and similar technologies.

The main data center providers are Google (Google Cloud), Microsoft (Azure), and Amazon (Amazon Web Services). They all offer integrated IoT and ML packages for data collection, analyses, and presentation. These data centers provide data storing and customized computation capacities for data analytics, by default, including ML capacities. There also are several open-source solutions for the more tech-savvy gardeners.

## Information Presentation

A great place to start is the ThingsBoard[27] open-source platform, which allows you to configure customizable IoT dashboards. Each IoT dashboard can contain multiple widgets that visualize data from various IoT devices. Once your lightweight IoT dashboard is created, you can assign it to numerous customers of your IoT project. Another popular open-source IoT platform is openBalena[28] which allows developers to manage their devices independently, mitigating lock-in fears and removing barriers to exit (and entry!).

Grafana[29] open source is one of the most popular visualization and analytics software platforms. It allows you to query, visualize, alert, and explore your metrics, logs and traces no matter where they are stored. It provides you with tools to turn your time-series database (TSDB) data into insightful graphs and visualizations.

## Raw Sentient Data Collection

Reliable data obtained from sensors able to read the plant's environment provides insights into the ten plant growth variables (and some additional information humans can't offer using only their senses).

- Ambient sensors—for measuring light levels, air pressure, humidity, and temperature

- Soil sensors—for measuring soil aeration, saturation levels, humidity, and temperature

- Optical sensors—offer hyperspectral, multispectral, fluorescence and thermal sensing

- Sensors for crop phenotyping—for monitoring plant growth and development

- Sensors for detection of microorganisms and pest management

- Sensors for detection and identification of crops and weeds

[top left] Five IBCs that collect rainwater from a roof, forming part of an 4,755-gallon (18,000-L) water catchment system at Simplify Gardening's garden. The containers are joined to allow rainwater to be pumped for irrigation use, helping to conserve water and reduce costs.

[top right] This compost pile, which until the photo was taken was covered by a tarp, is a result of natural breakdown of organic matter aided by beneficial microorganisms. Covering a compost pile with a tarp protects it from external elements and lets life and microbiology thrive.

[above] Here I am setting up drip irrigation in my polytunnel. Drip irrigation is a method of watering plants that involves delivering water directly to the roots, which helps to conserve water and promote healthy plant growth.

[right] Here, I am inserting a thermometer into a compost pile to monitor its temperature. This helps to ensure optimal conditions for decomposition and the growth of beneficial microorganisms.

In my polytunnel, I use homemade fertilizers while planting potatoes in containers, demonstrating my commitment to sustainable gardening practices and promoting self-sufficiency.

# Chapter 2:

## The Perfect Trio—
## Nature, Science, and You

Global climate changes require gardeners to become more agile in their approach to the craft. We all must draw alongside nature, forming a symbiotic relationship to help both flourish, even in challenging times. Extended droughts, higher temperatures, colder winters, floods—nature has an appropriate response, but humans need to listen. The average global temperature for September 2022, according to the National Oceanic and Atmospheric Administration (NOAA), was 1.58°F (0.88°C) higher than the 59.0°F (15.0°C) average for the twentieth century, making it tied with September 2021 for the fifth-warmest September since 1880. September 2022 was the forty-sixth consecutive September and the 453rd consecutive month, with temperatures above the average for the twentieth century.

Like any healthy relationship, we need to attune ourselves to the changing needs of the other, where, in the absence of steady rain, we help improve the soil's water-holding capacities. In floods, our soil needs improved cohesive strengths. While we often remember nature for her tempestuous display of force, the trick to becoming an effective gardener is to listen to her whispers. We must be present in the relationship, listening and responding—and nature will do the same; she always does. What are the plants and soil saying, the birds and the bees? Are there earthworms in the soil? Is the color of my plants' foliage changing—year after year after year? Are you attentive and finely sensitive to your garden's needs?

A healthy relationship is one where needs are met with finesse. Is it better to water more, or is it better to add microorganisms, mulch, and organic matter to help address the thirst? Do you rush in, adding nitrogen, insecticides, and everything you think your plant needs, or do you approach your garden with love and understanding? Nature loves natural solutions. In managing changing weather patterns, we need to work with nature, implementing subtle adjustments that prevent a pendulum swing from one extreme to the next.

In this chapter, you are the central character as we explore the pivotal role of nature, some of the science behind it, and your stewardship within the system. Let us briefly cover five concepts that will help us become better gardeners. Each of the five sections below offers you several challenges and opportunities to add experience to your knowledge.

- Systems awareness
- Ecological systems
- The adaptive cycle

- Biomimicry
- Applying systems thinking to gardening formats

## SYSTEMS AWARENESS

To help us understand systems better, let's consider the human body and the systems that keep us alive and (semi)-functional. Some of our systems include:

- Skeletal system
- Nervous system
- Circulatory system
- Respiratory system
- Digestive system

- Excretory system
- Integumentary system (e.g., skin, hair, nails, and exocrine glands)
- Endocrine system
- Reproductive system
- Lymphatic system

All these systems function only because they are part of the greater interdependent whole. That is what a system is: a collection of components and their relationship with other components within the system. When asked by their students when life began, Chilean biologists Humberto Maturana and Francisco Varela, after much thought, responded: "An autopoietic machine is a machine organized as a network of processes of production of components which: (i) through their interactions and transformations continuously regenerate and realize the network of processes that produced them; and (ii) constitute it as a concrete unity in space in which the components exist."[30] That's a mouthful way of saying that the first living system, some 3.8 billion years ago, was a separate entity that could sustain and grow itself from within (i.e., maintain its internal systems of functioning).

For such a system to exist, there needs to be some *communication*, biogeochemical interactions between parts of the system driven by needs and complex responses. Part of these systems are observable, but much of what happens is yet to be fully understood. Most of what we know is observed in the product rather than the process, noticing patterns, products, and perpetually evolving interactions. In a later section of this chapter, we'll look at biomimicry, the practice of emulating nature's systems in designs. We'll also explore how systems fluctuate between chaos and order, continuously redefining their expression in changing environments.

I regularly water my container potatoes in the polytunnel, where they are safeguarded from frost before the last frost date, ensuring their healthy growth and successful transition to the outdoor garden.

[top] This close-up image of an earthworm wriggling on a nutrient-rich compost pile, showcases the essential role these humble creatures play in breaking down organic matter and improving soil fertility in gardens.

[bottom] A disheartening image of wilting herbs, visibly suffering from a lack of water, serving as a reminder of the importance of proper hydration in maintaining the health and vitality of plants in our gardens.

[page right] There are several systems that influence the way a plant grows.

## PATTERNS

A pattern is a recurring trait that helps identify a phenomenon within a system. We sneeze in reflex to prevent any undesired stimulus from getting into the upper-respiratory tract—a respiratory system mechanism. The main driving force is the pressure induced by the spasmodic contraction of internal intercostal and abdominal muscles. There's a pattern to it. We smell because our olfactory receptor cells adapt to the odor's molecule shape. The change causes us to notice the smell, but constant exposure to a smell causes us to notice it no longer, as there is no status change to the olfactory receptors.

Patterns may be physical or behavioral, such as beehive honeycombs or gnats flying in your face in pursuit of the $CO_2$ you exhale. Natural patterns become more unpredictable as variables increase. Emergent properties become observable as the relationships between the system elements and the environment strengthen. An example is the abundance of earthworms in your soil, a soil-health indicator. Some manifestations of system dynamics are more complex. When leaves wilt, we know they have lost water pressure (turgidity), but the cause may need a broader system review; drought could cause wilting leaves, but so too could a fungal infection compromising the xylem's ability to supply the leaves with water (often caused by overwatering).

The wilting leaf example highlights nature's feedback loops, where we can see something is wrong but will need to look at other components in the system to determine the actual cause. Multiple feedback loops are present to indicate a plant's health, though not all of them are visible. Feedback loops also serve the plants in other ways. A Philodendron has a skototropic response to dark shapes on its horizon. Unlike other phototropic plants that grow toward the light, the philodendron grows toward the dark figure on the horizon in search of a tree to climb (Philo—friend; dendron—tree).

Back to the wilting leaves, unless you check the plant roots for rot, you would not be wrong to think that your wilting plant is dehydrated, but your error would be that you are not considering the whole system. Of course, not all feedback from the system is negative. If our tomato plant is vigorous and carries 30 pounds (14 kg) of tomatoes, you know your system is functioning optimally. Natural systems tend to be in constant flux, self-organizing into structures that best ensure stability. We'll explore these in more detail in the adaptive cycles section below.

## Ecological Systems

There is a field of science known as the ecological systems theory applied to human development, specifically psychology and child development (i.e., ecosystemic psychology). It is interesting in that it helps people understand the effects adverse childhood experiences (ACEs)[31] have on people throughout their lives. Though that sphere of science interests me greatly, this section is not about that. Instead, let's explore the environmental systems influencing our plants' health.

A plant's life is subject to several systems that affect its growth, development, and productivity. These are the air (atmosphere), water (hydrosphere), the earth below (lithosphere), and interactions with other living organisms (biosphere). Central to these four is the pedosphere, directly translated, the land upon which we tread, the planet's surface.

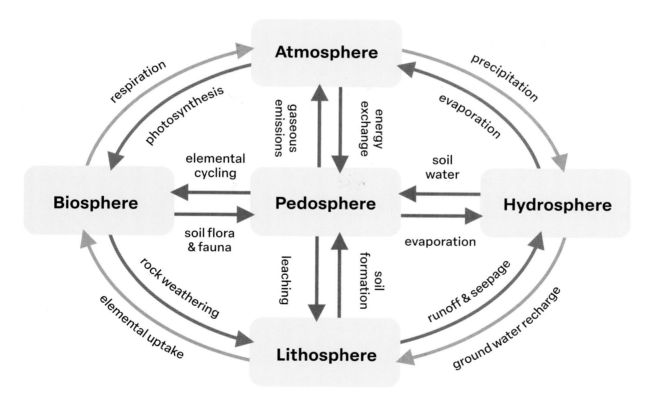

**Layers of the Atmosphere**

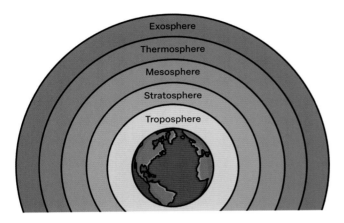

## *The Atmosphere*

We've already covered some atmospheric characteristics, especially their impact on global warming. The atmospheric system consists of 78 percent nitrogen, 21 percent oxygen, less than a percent argon, and a mere 0.04 percent carbon dioxide, just enough to insulate the Earth from extreme day/night temperature variances. The atmosphere is a dynamic system with a higher density of gases at sea level, decreasing the higher you go. The bottom 6.2 miles (10 km)—the troposphere—contains about 90 percent of the atmospheric gases. Above that, between 6.2 and 31 miles (10 and 50 km), we have the stratosphere, which commercial airlines use due to low air resistance. In the 18.6 miles (30 km) above that, the mesosphere can reach temperatures of -148°F (-100°C). Earth is the third warmest planet in the solar system, mainly because of its unique atmospheric composition. The line is fine; too little $CO_2$ in the atmosphere would see us freezing, while too much would create an ultraviolet (UV) light oven.

As a system, the atmosphere's interaction with other systems is uniquely significant:

### Hydrosphere ↔ Atmosphere
This interaction includes moisture exchange (precipitation and evaporation), with several interacting systems influenced by:

- Earth's rotation on its axis and the resultant centrifugal force affects wind direction. Varying surface temperatures across the globe also influence wind direction. Earth's rotation also is responsible for the circadian cycle regulating plant transpiration, photosynthesis, and even reproductive fertility cycles.

- Regional angles to the sun at different times of the year (a single orbit of Earth's trip around the sun), especially toward the Arctic (northernmost) and Antarctic (southernmost) regions. The Earth's 23.5-degree angle tilt across its rotation axis is responsible for our annual changing proximity to the sun, summer and winter. The areas between the Tropic of Capricorn (south) and the Tropic of Cancer (north) are less affected by the axial tilt.

- Varying land and sea temperatures

- Air pollution levels

### Atmosphere ↔ Biosphere
This interaction provides gases for respiration and access to energy from the sun. It also absorbs evapotranspiration from the biosphere.

### Atmosphere ↔ Pedosphere
This interaction is absorbing gases and exchanging energy. A symbiotic relationship between plants and microorganisms allows the pedosphere to store carbon dioxide, extract nitrogen, and increase the atmosphere's oxygen levels.

### Atmosphere ↔ Lithosphere
This interaction exchanges heat, buffers surface temperature variations, and causes rock degradation and soil formation.

**The Water Cycle**

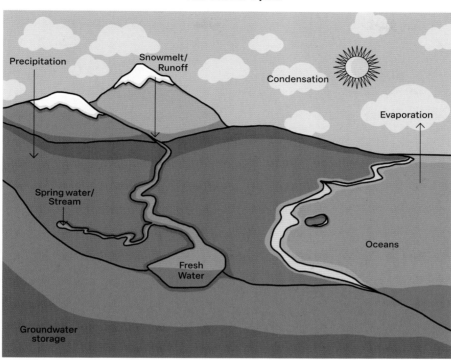

### The Hydrosphere

The hydrosphere isn't a continuous system and includes underground water bodies, surface water bodies, rivers, seas, glaciers, and water within the atmosphere. It consists of planet Earth's gaseous, liquid, and solid water. The hydrosphere stretches from the lithosphere into the atmosphere, including the pedosphere. The biosphere depends on it for life, though some organisms can survive without it for extended periods. Humans can live without food for about three weeks, without water for about three days, and without air for about three minutes. Most of the water in the atmosphere is in a gaseous form, and as it rises and cools, it condenses to form clouds for precipitation back down.

According to USDA[32], only 2.5 percent of all the water on the planet is not saline, and only 1.2 percent of that 2.5 percent is available as surface water, i.e., 0.03 percent. A further 30.1 percent of freshwater can be found underground, and the remaining 68.7 percent is tied up in glaciers and ice caps. Water is finite, and we must treat it with the utmost respect.

From a systems perspective, this is how the hydrosphere interacts with other systems:

#### Hydrosphere ↔ Lithosphere

Consider the Grand Canyon and other examples of water's current and past action on the Earth's surface.

#### Hydrosphere ↔ Biosphere

Without water, the biosphere will not survive for long, as plants and animals depend on a constant supply of fresh water. We will explore its role in a later chapter, where we look at different watering strategies.

#### Hydrosphere ↔ Pedosphere

The pedosphere is the Earth's soil cover and is about 6.5 feet (2 m) thick. The pedosphere's ability to hold water depends on its particle size and cation exchange capacity (CEC), a product of the organic content in the mix. A higher organic content generally means a more diverse population of microorganisms, which also add to the soil's water-holding capacity—more on this later.

### The Lithosphere

According to NASA, the Earth's equatorial circumference is 24,873.6 miles (~40,000 km), and the surface area is 196,936,994 square miles (510,000,000 sq km). A mountain such as Mount Everest, that's 5.5 miles (8.8 km) high, is hardly a blip in the greater scheme of things.

The lithosphere comprises the outermost 62.14 miles (100 km) of the Earth's solid surface and entails the crust and the higher, more brittle part of the mantle. The lithosphere is the layer of Earth that is the coldest and the most unyielding.

Tectonic activity is the most well-known aspect of the Earth's lithosphere. The movement and collision of these enormous lithosphere plates are known as tectonic activity. Africa, Antarctica, Australia, Eurasia, India, Juan de Fuca, North America, South America, Scotia, Philippines, Pacific, Cocos, and Nazca are just a few of the fifteen major tectonic plates that make up the lithosphere.

From a systems perspective, this is how the lithosphere interacts with other systems:

#### Lithosphere ↔ Pedosphere

Earth's thin fertile crust, the pedosphere, is a product of weathering of rocks and sedimentation formed over the millennia. Water and its dissolved content leach into the lithosphere.

#### Lithosphere ↔ Biosphere

The exchange between the two is mainly chemical, with the rock releasing elements and microorganisms aiding its decomposition.

**Layering of the Earth**

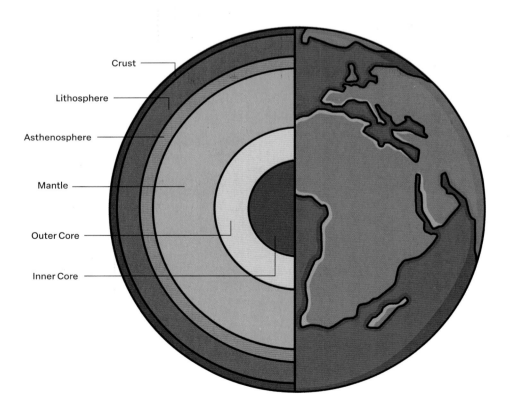

Crust
Lithosphere
Asthenosphere
Mantle
Outer Core
Inner Core

**Biosphere**

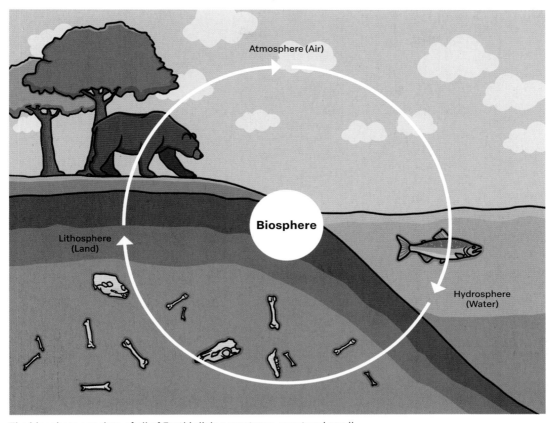

The biosphere consists of all of Earth's living creatures, great and small.

## *The Biosphere*

The biosphere includes all of Earth's animals, plants, and an array of organisms, including humans. These ecological communities interact with the Earth's physical aspects, including the pedosphere, hydrosphere, lithosphere, and atmosphere.

Collectively, we refer to these ecological communities as biomes. There are five levels of biomes, each defined by the regional temperatures. We can further classify each group by water availability. Thus, we have:

- Arctic regions
- Tundra biome
- Subarctic regions
- Coniferous forests (boreal forest biome)
- Temperate regions
- The temperate deciduous forest biome
- Chaparral biome

- Grassland biome
- Desert biome
- Tropical regions
- Tropical rainforest biome
- Tropical seasonal forest biome
- Scrubland biome
- Savannah biome

Each biome system has different survival mechanisms with tiered trophic levels in the food chain—a means of energy transference. The main source of energy is the sun, and it helps produce life in plants. Predator and prey cycles, life and death, transfers of energy, ending with microorganisms responsible for returning the unspent energy to the primary energy converters, plants. The biosphere ranges from heights of up to 41,000 feet (12,500 m) above sea level to depths of at least 26,247 feet (8,000 m) in the ocean. There is fossilized evidence of a functional biosphere some 3.8 billion years ago.

The University of Arizona has an extensive biosphere laboratory called Biosphere 2.[33] It is a 3.14 acres (1.27 ha) enclosure consisting of 7.2 million cubic feet (203,881 m³) of sealed glass using 6,500 windows and standing 91 feet (27.7 m) tall at its highest point. The facility allows the university to mimic a 20,000-square foot (1,858 m²) rainforest, modeled on the Venezuelan rainforest biospheres. Several other installations are on the 40-acre (~16 ha) campus in the Sonoran Desert.

From a systems perspective, here is a system's dependency on the biosphere not yet covered:

### Biosphere ↔ Pedosphere

The pedosphere is a product of the lithosphere's oxidation, the weathering of rocks and sedimentation formed over the millennia. Water and its dissolved content can leach into the lithosphere.

### *The Pedosphere*

Pedos as in pedal and pedestrian, but not the Spanish *pedos*, which means to flatulate. Those few feet that cover the Earth's surface, the depth of a grave, are home to most of Earth's life. Plants, the most dominant species by far, root in the pedosphere, which hosts the next most prevalent species, soil fungi first, and then soil bacteria.[34] Humans, by the way, are about ninth on the list of dominant numbers, after livestock and before wild mammals—meaning there are more humans than rodents, but about three times as many chickens as people.

As gardeners, we're very interested in the pedosphere, its interaction with other ecological systems, and the systems it hosts, such as the soil food web. We're curious how it manages chemical elements, especially plant nutrients, aggregation, drainage, water retention, aeration, and all the things that make plants thrive.

Soil organisms serve numerous roles in the pedosphere. Their most critical function is the regulation of biogeochemical transformations. Five functions mediated by the soil biota are:

- Improved soil structure by aggregate formation
- Soil organic matter processing, including carbon mineralization and sequestration
- Nutrient cycling
- Pathogenic interaction, including disease prevention and transmission
- Degradation of pollutants and toxins
- Symbiotic relationships

Some greenhouse gases (GHG), notably carbon dioxide ($CO_2$), methane ($CH_4$), and nitrous oxide ($N_2O$), are produced as byproducts of metabolic oxidation, depending on the soil's oxygen levels. Autotrophic mineralization is microbial activities that regulate GHG emissions through the oxidation and reduction of carbon and nitrogen. Soil management practices affect these processes, including nitrogen fertilizer, tillage, water usage, pesticide usage, and herbicide usage.

The pedosphere is the only system that directly interacts with the other four systems, atmosphere, biosphere, lithosphere, and hydrosphere:

**The pedosphere's effect on the atmosphere:** There is some gas exchange, but this is mainly due to the biosphere's activity in the pedosphere.

**The atmosphere's effect on the pedosphere:** The atmosphere is responsible for heating the pedosphere, a transference of initial energy to sustain life.

**The pedosphere's effect on the biosphere:** The pedosphere acts as plant anchorage and a conduit for nutritional elements and hydration. It also hosts the three most abundant living organisms: trees, fungi, and bacteria.

**The biosphere's effect on the pedosphere:** The biosphere is the pedosphere's source of life, essential to its effective functioning.

**The pedosphere's effect on the lithosphere:** The pedosphere acts as a lithosphere decomposer, breaking rocks down into complex elements that the biosphere further processes into bioavailable nutrients.

**The lithosphere's effect on the pedosphere:** The lithosphere is the pedosphere's foundation and essential material supplier.

**The pedosphere's effect on the hydrosphere:** The pedosphere holds water and releases some as evaporation.

**The hydrosphere's effect on the pedosphere:** The hydrosphere is essential to the pedosphere's functioning as a water supply.

## Pedosphere

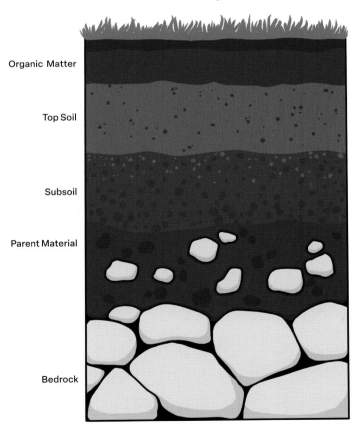

Organic Matter

Top Soil

Subsoil

Parent Material

Bedrock

The pedosphere is the ecological system that most impacts plant growth below ground.

A garden can only produce as much as the available resources will allow. Provide your garden with the resources it needs, and you'll reap the benefits.

### Adaptive Cycles

According to biblical accounts, chaos is the birthplace of order, the wellspring of all. The adaptive cycles model[35], first defined by Gunderson and Holling (2001), helps us visualize the interplay between chaos and order and the forces or behaviors contributing to growth and collapse cycles. It reminds me of David Olson's FACES IV (Family Adaptability and Cohesion Evaluation Scale)[36], which helps families identify their levels of flexibility (rigidity vs. chaos) and cohesion (disengaged vs. enmeshed). Balancing these four tensions helps families live happier lives. There must be enough chaos for creativity and innovation while maintaining order. On the other plane, individuals in the family need to temper their clinginess with respect for the other's individuality and right to autonomy without becoming totally disengaged. A central element is bidirectional communication.

The adaptive cycle model includes systems destabilization and reorganization processes, often neglected in favor of growth and conservation. By having inverted development (destruction and reorganization) processes, a holistic view of the system dynamics, organization, and resilience can be considered.

An essential element for understanding complex systems is an appreciation of their inherent instability, alternating between growth and stability followed by sudden collapse and reinvention. Four activities divide the adaptive cycle into two phases, growth and conservation, followed by a collapse and reinvention.

### Growth or Exploitation

Whether a society, a community, or a garden, growth and expansion depend on a) the optimal access (exploitation) and use of the available resources, and b) building selective relationships that strengthen capacities and minimize risks. Relationship stability requires some order, either cultivated or enforced. In a garden, this means that in the absence of reasonable diversity, some organisms (pathogens) or plants (weeds) may dominate to the exclusion of others. Resilience is a product of diversity, creating checks and balances within the system.

### Conservation

Once dominance is achieved, the strong rule over the weak. Order is maintained, and the focus is on accumulating resources that benefit the dominators. Established give-and-take relationships strengthen the system's framework, limiting instability and stifling innovation and change. The system's most vigorous drive is self-preservation by maximally exploiting available resources and excluding anything threatening the system's stability and growth.

### Collapse

Contrary to the supposition[37] that exploitation can be endlessly perpetuated, at some point, the system collapses due to its unsustainability or internal forces that eventually collaborate to end the tyranny. The unchecked growth of a plantation finally shuts out any sun to the forest floor, meaning plants die and are susceptible to fires. The ensuing fire causes the established plantation to collapse and regenerates the growth of the weaker organisms.

### Reorganization

The new system is a blank canvas of opportunity. Components of the collapsed system with the most resilience are likely to thrive. It is a season for innovative and novel ways of doing things, unencumbered by failed rules and filled with learning from previous failures. In these times, animal behavior changes, plants with resilient traits emerge, and communities draw on social memory to facilitate new growth (and exploitation).

### Adaptive Cycle Example

Let's take a fire as an example; after all, I am a firefighter. There is a grass field with some trees. From afar, the whole plot is a relatively stable system. Then a fire burns the grass to stubs, singes the lower branches, and burns the outer bark. Some rodents fail to escape, and the topsoil is scorched.

We now have an altered system that appears destroyed but is a blank slate of potential. The grass has established roots, but it has limited foliage to feed and hydrate. The trees' roots are unharmed, and they, too, have less to feed after the loss of some branches. The partially burnt bark still has xylem and phloem channels in place. The strongest rodents and insects are likely to survive. The system is at a point where the most vigorous plants and animals will exploit the void left by the fire—the system's potential.

After the first rain or moisture, the blackened field bursts into life, supported by established root systems. It looks like it's raining green, the sheer speed of exploitation.

Subsystems that are most effective at forming connections with other elements grow faster and more robust.

A study[38] showed that some fungi (*Rhizophagus irregularis* and *Serendipita bescii*) actively help some bacteria survive droughts. As the plants grow, they flourish, as does the rest of the soil food web. Eventually, the system achieves some form of equilibrium (order). But a state of order is less flexible, and any onslaught can move the system from a state of conservation to a state of release and reorganization—until the next calamity.

Birth, development, maturity, and death are the four phases the system goes through. Death is the passing of the baton to the next generation of living organisms. Gardeners annually reorganize a system's structure and operations during the destruction and reorganization phases. Keeping the soil intact and allowing some plants that have shown resilience in adverse conditions builds the overall system's resilience, retaining some systems learning. To reduce the danger to the overall structure, we insert mutations in the adaptive cycle and purposefully rearrange the system. We will explore how we do this as we survey the different gardening formats later in this chapter.

Natural areas that have been subjected to wildfires regenerate and eventually achieve some form of equilibrium.

### Biomimicry

I'm unsure how long it took for our prehistoric ancestors to learn that foraging and hunting could be made more accessible by animal domestication and gardening. The book of Genesis says Cain chose gardening, and his brother, Abel, chose livestock, so I imagine it was ages ago that we decided to mimic nature in some way. I'm interested in how far we can go in seeing what nature does and how it does it and doing the same. It's not so simple, as the Wright brothers would tell you if they were here.

You may find two sister websites of particular interest: biomimicry.org and asknature.org. They are both quite inspirational. Biomimicry teaches us to see the world with compassion, helping us better comprehend the interdependent web of life and our place in it. Taking cues from the methods employed by existing species allows us to improve our own way of doing things. In nature, the systems that don't work have self-eliminated. To solve our most significant design challenges in a way that is both sustainable and in solidarity with all species on Earth, we must develop new products, processes, systems, or ways of living. By imitating nature's strategies, we can benefit from her insights and apply them to heal ourselves and the Earth.

### *The Success Factor—YOU!*

While no single element in a system is more important than another, humans have special significance because of their strength and their potential effect on other parts of the system. You are a pivotal part of what happens around you, and your knowledge, skills, and behavior are vitally important in shaping your environment. How you exercise your volition can make or break a system.

We get the energy we need to live from the nutrition we consume, and irrespective of your preferred diet, the atmosphere, hydrosphere, biosphere, and pedosphere are pivotal to its availability. How you use these systems' life-giving components depends on your understanding of their respective role within your chosen system for plant growth.

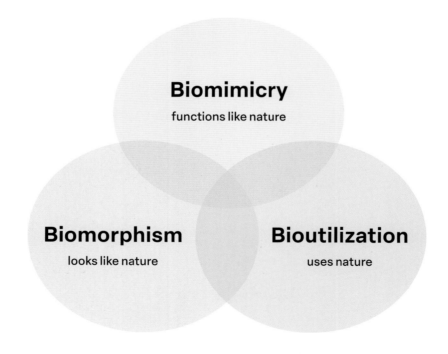

A triad of imitating nature's strategies

## APPLYING SYSTEMS THINKING TO GARDENING FORMATS

Let us now explore systems thinking in the context of four diverse gardening formats:

- Traditional in-ground vegetable gardens

- Raised beds

- Vertical gardens

- Hydroponics

### In-Ground Vegetable Gardening

The most crucial aspects to consider when choosing a garden location are:

- Sunlight, nitrogen, oxygen, and carbon dioxide—Atmosphere

- Access to water and the site's ability to manage water—Hydrosphere

- Mineral composition, structure, carbon content—Pedosphere

- The soil's biodiversity, surrounding plants, and biological threats—Biosphere

- The soil depth and composition—Lithosphere

### *Atmosphere—Sunlight, Nitrogen, Oxygen, and Carbon Dioxide*

#### Sunlight

Different plants need different levels of sunlight; generally, fruit-bearing plants such as the Solanaceae family (e.g., tomatoes, eggplants, peppers, potatoes), the Cucurbitaceae family (e.g., squashes, gourds, cucumber, pumpkins), and the Fabaceae family (e.g., peas, beans, soybeans) love full sun.

Some veggies are more tolerant of shade than others, such as the Brassicaceae family (e.g., cabbage, cauliflower, kale, radishes), the Apiaceae family (e.g., carrots, celery, parsley, parsnip), and the Asteraceae family (e.g., lettuce, endives, artichokes).

Being a responsible steward of your garden—and your world—is important to fostering a balanced ecosystem.

[top] Standing amid an array of vibrant, healthy vegetables grown directly in the garden soil, showcases the fruits of my labor and the potential of traditional gardening practices for bountiful harvests.

[bottom] I can't help but proudly pose beside a massive pumpkin I successfully cultivated in my garden, demonstrating my expertise in growing techniques and passion for producing extraordinary, eye-catching produce.

### Nitrogen

Nitrogen is the most abundant gas in the atmosphere, but plants need a symbiotic relationship with microorganisms to access atmospheric nitrogen. *Rhizobium* bacteria penetrate the roots forming nodules that fix and convert atmospheric nitrogen to ammonia. The ammonia is then converted by the plant to amino acids and proteins, leading to increased crop yield and seed protein levels in the case of legumes. Scientists are discovering that mycorrhizal symbiosis, the relationship between a nitrogen-fixating fungus and plant roots, extends to interplant communication and support networks. Do yourself a favor and search "The Secret Language of Trees" on YouTube.[39]

### Oxygen and Carbon Dioxide

Atmospheric carbon dioxide ($CO_2$) levels are only 0.04 percent, so much of the plant's $CO_2$ consumption depends on soil microbial carbon decomposition activities that release $CO_2$ as the main by-product. Photosynthesis uses sunlight energy to convert water and carbon dioxide into glucose, oxygen, and water. Conversely, plant respiration uses oxygen and glucose, produces carbon dioxide, and releases water and energy. A function of respiration is adenosine triphosphate (ATP) production, a molecule essential in several metabolic reactions in plant cells, including photosynthesis.

### Airflow

Another critical factor to consider is enough airflow. Avoid putting the garden in a low-lying area, such as at the bottom of a slope. These locations are slow to warm in the spring, and frost accumulates more easily because cold air gathers at the lowest point and cannot drain away. Vegetable gardens on higher ground are less likely to be affected by mild freezes, allowing for an earlier start in the spring and a more prolonged harvest in the fall.

## Hydrosphere—Water and Water Management

It also is critical to have good soil drainage. Examine your yard after rain—areas where water pools have poor drainage and would not be suitable for a garden without extensive rehabilitation. When deciding where to put your garden, consider the ease of access to quality water sources. Access to a water point or irrigation system eliminates the need to transport water during the dry months.

Soil water management capacities are greatly improved by a diverse population of microorganisms, but more on this later. Also, consider using a 50-gallon (189-L) tank and drip irrigation using a solar-powered pump. The ideal, of course, would be to incorporate a soil moisture meter that triggers the pump only when needed. Using water that has stood for a while lessens the impact of fluoride and chlorine.

Don't build your garden where water pools. Poor drainage impedes plant growth.

Use a leguminous cover crop as your first planting to help increase soil organic matter and nitrogen.

### Pedosphere—Soil Tilth, Carbon Content, and Microbial Activity

Essential indicators of soil health are the levels of stable carbon content, tilth, chemical composition, and biological activity.

### Carbon Content

Excessive uncomposted carbon matter means that microorganisms need nitrogen to decompose the carbon, and they get preferred access to the available nitrogen. It is best to compost carbon-rich materials before adding them to your soil. If this is impractical, i.e., the ground already has significant levels of plant residue in the soil, plant a nitrogen fixer such as clover for a season before using the area as a garden. Carbon content is essential for microbial life, so don't veer off to the opposite end of the spectrum. A carbon-free site is most unhealthy for in-ground gardens.

### Tilth

Look for surface crusting, ponding, and penetration resistance. These are indicators that the soil is compacted. Compost is the best solution for compacted soil, often used for restoration on construction and mining sites. Compost contains microorganisms that attract tilth engineers such as earthworms that function as aggregate and pore developers for improved drainage and water-holding capacities. If you have time, cover the planned bed with 4 inches (10 cm) of compost and allow it to stand for at least six months before planting. If you have time constraints, dig the compost into the top 6 inches (15 cm) of a fallow bed. Let your first crop always be legumes, as they fix atmospheric nitrogen for use by subsequent crops, produce biomass, add organic matter to the soil, prevent erosion and compaction, and attract beneficial insects. Possible options include[40]:

- Winter annuals, such as field peas, crimson clover, hairy vetch, and several others

- Biennials, such as sweet clover

- Perennials, such as white clover or red clover

- Summer annuals (grow winter annuals in the summer of colder regions)

### Chemical Composition

Soil testing provides valuable information on pH and plant-available nutrients. Test your soil before planting and every two to three years after that; inexpensive soil-test kits are unreliable. Use a reputable agency or local Extension office to accurately determine your soil characteristics. Some tests can even provide a breakdown of the microbial populations in your soil.

### Biosphere—Soil Biodiversity

Biota diversity is essential in keeping soils healthy and productive. Irresponsible soil and plant management practices ignore the work done by soil organisms. Using pesticides, herbicides, and overfertilization significantly contribute to rising rates of land degradation, nutrient depletion, fertility decline, water shortages, and yield reductions. Managing soil biological processes and employing measures that promote activity can preserve and enhance soil fertility.

First and foremost, soil organisms require food (carbon), enough moisture, and protection from chemical and mechanical stresses. When comparing locations where deep tillage is used with shallow tillage, ridge tillage, or no-tillage and surface management of crop residues, it is common to find that the latter has higher levels of earthworm activity. Because of their potential to improve plant development and preserve soil quality, earthworms are a valuable resource for your garden.

### Lithosphere—Soil Composition and Structure

Undisturbed natural soils typically consist of three distinctly sized layers. Layers include the parent material (lithosphere), topsoil, and subsoil. There may be two or more horizons inside a given layer, which are the soil profile's building blocks.

A healthy soil is alive with life, both visible and microscopic.

# Raised Bed Vegetable Gardening

## On-Ground Raised Beds

These garden areas are elevated 6 to 8 inches (15 to 20 cm) above the ground level. They are linked to the native soil underneath them, and they may or may not have built sides. Raised beds can be created by changing the local topography, digging walkways, and using the soil to lift the beds higher than the surrounding landscape. They can be framed with logs, boulders, wooden boards, or straw bales. Raised beds with just enough width to reach the middle are great for producing veggies. Defined beds make a garden more appealing and limit cross-contamination. Raised beds drain better and can warm up faster, extending the growing season.

## Lifted Raised Beds

You may need more soil if you're building a taller raised bed or one in a framed box. If your soil is of excellent quality loam, you may screen it into the raised bed and mix it with 50 percent compost. Raised garden soil mixtures can be purchased from a nursery. Consider that 1 cubic yard (0.76 m³) of soil equals 27 cubic feet (765 L) when calculating how many square yards (m³) you require.

The soil used inside the beds can be altered to suit plant needs. Generally, higher organic content increases cation exchange capacities (CEC), more on this later, and it improves water-holding potential. Adding inert materials such as pumice, expanded shale, or vermiculite enhances drainage. You can achieve optimized saturation porosity and field capacity levels by balancing organic and inorganic materials.

Avoid cedar and walnut in raised bed construction as both have pesticide properties and can negatively impact your soil's microorganism populations. While these woods are more rot-resistant, they will negatively affect your crops. Do not use treated pine either—such as wood from pallets. Wrapping your lumber in weed cloth can extend its life by up to ten years, and untreated lumber should last six years.

Off the ground, raised beds must have drainage holes to prevent plant roots from standing in water and causing root rot. Using pebbles at the bottom of the pot or container is not advised. Contrary to popular belief, they serve no purpose and create more risks than benefits. Raised beds should be between 12 and 18 inches (30 and 45 cm) deep to accommodate a selection of plants. Annual plants and vegetables with shallow roots, such as lettuce, radishes, and scallions, require a potting mix depth of 6 to 8 inches (15 to 20 cm). Most herbs may be grown in raised beds subdivided into 6-inch (15-cm) squares.

I like being resourceful. Here, I'm standing between two sturdy and visually appealing raised beds I constructed using reclaimed decking boards and corrugated tin sheeting, exemplifying my commitment to sustainability and innovative garden design.

## Vertical Gardening

Vertical gardening involves trellises, poles, tiered beds, and strings to support growing plants. This strategy is ideal for gardeners with limited gardening space or arable land. Tomatoes, cucumbers, melons, pole beans, and other vining plants are suitable for vertical planting. Some plants weave themselves onto the framework, while others require tying.

Vertical plants throw a shadow, so put them on the north side of a garden bed to avoid shadowing and grow shade-tolerant crops nearby. Vertically grown plants take up considerably less space, and while the yield per plant is lower, the yield per square foot is significantly higher.

Vertically growing plants are more exposed to the elements, causing them to dry out faster—remember to compensate for the loss by watering more regularly. This rapid drying is beneficial to plants that are prone to fungal infections. Raised, tiered beds are typically used in vertical gardening.

[top] This charming raised bed is crafted from stones dug from the garden, which now serves as a flourishing herb garden. The photo highlights the resourceful use of natural materials to create functional and sustainable garden structures.

[left] A robust bean support structure is fastened with zip ties, illustrating the benefits of growing vertically to maximize garden space and promote efficient use of available resources for bountiful harvests.

[top] Growing hydroponically at home isn't for everyone, but if you have the space and are willing to learn, hydroponic growing can produce a lot of food.

[bottom] Deep water culture home hydroponics is straightforward and easy to DIY.

# Hydroponics

There are two categories of hydroponic systems: liquid and aggregate. Plant roots float freely in a liquid system unsupported by a growing medium. In an aggregate approach, the roots grow in an inert medium through which water moves freely. Aggregate systems may use active or passive water-supply systems.

Hydroponic systems are further divided into open and closed systems, referring to nutrient usage. Open systems use nutrition-laden water once, while closed systems continuously recycle water and replenish nutrients as needed.

As mentioned earlier, aggregate systems use passive and active strategies for water delivery. The passive approach doesn't require pumps that create a flow of water over the plant roots but instead uses a high capillary action wick to transport the water to the roots.[41]

## *Types of Hydroponic Gardening Systems*

Below is a review of the six most common hydroponic garden systems. I also expand on hydroponic systems you can affordably use at home.

## *Deep Water Culture (Home-use Winner)*

Also known as the floating platform or water culture system, it has a polystyrene platform that allows the plant roots to remain partially submerged in nutrient-enriched water. An air pump continuously forces air for water aeration.

This is the most straightforward hydroponic system to use at home and can often be bought as a kit. All you need to make your own is a deep-bottomed container, an air pump, and an air stone (and connecting pipes).

Each plant is placed in a perforated cup or a special basket (net cups) that fits into round slots cut into the polystyrene board, allowing part of the plant's roots to dangle in the water.

I prefer using coconut coir as an anchorage for the plant in the net cup, but perlite, clay pellets (Hydroton®), or pumice, are all popular alternatives. NASA uses coconut coir, or a special fertilizer-infused silica clay called arcillite[42], with a naturally high cation exchange capacity (CEC), for their space station tests.

The deep water culture system also is the least expensive and easiest to maintain and expand the hydroponic gardening system.

### *A Step-by-Step Guide to Making Your Own Deep Water Culture Hydroponics System*

Make sure the Styrofoam™ has enough room to move up and down by cutting it to fit the container.

Add at least 5 inches (12.5 cm) of water to the container, keeping track of how much you add.

For each gallon (3.8 L) of water used in the hydroponic garden, add 2 teaspoons (10 ml) of water-soluble fertilizer, such as a balanced 20–20–20 fertilizer with micronutrients.

Add Epsom salts (magnesium sulfate) to the water at a rate of a teaspoon per gallon.

Cut 2.5-inch (6-cm) holes into polystyrene boards for 3-inch (7.5-cm) net pots or 1.75-inch (4.5-cm) holes for 2-inch (5-cm) net pots. Pot size selection is based on the mature plant's expected stem girth. Net cups should not stick out and should fit snugly into the polystyrene board.

Space holes 12 inches (30 cm) apart and 6 inches (15 cm) from the sides.

Stake seedlings with toothpicks and plant them with some of the initial germination soil. Ensure there is an opportunity for the roots to access water without being totally submerged—they still need to breathe.

Maintain the water level by adding water that has been preconfigured with the required nutrients. Hydroponic gardening is an excellent way for children (and adults) to observe how temperatures, light, and humidity affect a plant's water use.

I grow my outdoor hydroponic garden under a 30 to 50 percent shade cloth and closely monitor water levels after a downpour. I adjust the nutrients accordingly if the rain adds quite a bit of water.

The water culture system is an open system, meaning that I discard my hydroponic garden's used water onto my garden beds after every harvest or two. Without a doubt, this is the most effortless gardening I've ever done.

A DIY deep water hydroponic system.

## NFT System (Nutrient Film Technique)

The nutrient film system is one of the most common hydroponic systems, maybe only second to the ebb and flow system. Both use gravity as their primary flow system, allowing nutrition-laden water to flow over the plant's root tips enabling the plants to grow.

Water and essential elements are monitored and continually adjusted in this closed-loop system. Micropumps connected to dissolved nutrient concentrates adjust the levels of all nineteen essential plant nutrients on the run. The nutrient film technique allows growing plants to absorb their required nutrients, and because the environment is uniform, plant growth is uniform too.

### *Ebb and Flow System*

As I said, the ebb and flow system is similar to the NFT system. Water flows through sealed pipes that prevent airborne contaminants from entering the system. Holes in pipes and ducts give plant roots access to the nutrient solution.

As the name suggests, the difference in this hydroponic system, unlike the NFT system, is that the water supply is intermittent. The timed pump switches on and off at different intervals, catering to a plant's varying day and night water needs.

We know plants grow because of photosynthesis, using water, $CO_2$, and light to make glucose. The ebb and flow method gives the plant more water when the lights are on and less when the lights are off. Light variation plays a vital role in flowering plants, though a few plants (e.g., tomatoes) are not affected by photoperiodism—but more on that in chapter 3.

Most plants tend to have a circadian cycle, where day and night are linked to growth and flowering cycles, which varies for different plants. Hydroponic plants benefit from getting what they need when they need it, including nutrients, light levels, and water. Even $CO_2$ levels are substituted for a fast-growing plant and generally kept under LED grow lights.

### *The Drip System*

A continuous or intermittent water flow over the root tips represents the liquid category of hydroponics. The drip system is an aggregate system and uses pipes to drip water onto the aggregate for access by growing plants. Plants grown in an aggregate have particular pH requirements, and the system uses tiny tubes that risk blocking. Still, the drip system is arguably the most widely used system for hydroponic growing. Like the previous system, it too

Here I am diligently setting up a gravity-powered, automated watering, autopot system in the polytunnel. My adoption of hydroponic technology has become a means to achieve consistently impressive harvests and optimize garden productivity.

is timer controlled and drips nutrient solution onto the base of each plant via a small drip line.

### Wick System

The wick system relies on capillary action to draw water from a reservoir to the plant roots. While I've read that it is best suited for smaller plants such as lettuce, foresters[43] use the wick system, complete with biodegradable reservoirs, to establish saplings. The wick system is exceptionally viable in environments where growing plants is challenging, such as deserts, where it's used to establish palms. Though not a transitional hydroponics system, the tree establishment project uses this ingenious system to provide plants with enough water to develop their root systems.

### Aeroponics System

The aeroponic system is probably the most high-tech solution to growing soilless plants. This hydroponics system uses nutrient solution misters to irrigate the roots, and the only growing medium is in the net pots. Misting cycles are timer controlled, much like other types of hydroponics systems. The aeroponic system needs a short cycle timer that runs the nutrient solution pump for a few seconds every couple of minutes.

Most indoor hydroponics systems require extensive capital investment to provide the optimal environment, including an intelligent lighting system. The benefit is that every aspect of the plant's growth can be monitored, and interventions are done remotely via control panels. There is no distinct labeling for hydroponically grown vegetables in the Netherlands, where hydropic gardening is the leading agricultural system.

Next, we'll take a look at the many factors involved in providing your vegetable plants with what they need to thrive and produce maximum yields.

These tomatoes flourishing all year round inside a grow tent, are expertly maintained under energy-efficient LED lighting, exemplifying the potential of modern growing techniques to extend the traditional growing season.

Optimizing plant growth is the result of providing your plants with everything they need to thrive.

# Chapter 3:
## Optimizing Plant Growth

Every plant has fundamental needs that must be met for optimal growth. The better you can meet those needs, the healthier the plant will be, and healthy plants produce healthy crops in abundance. Essentially eleven factors influence plant growth and development efficacy: five above-the-ground and five in-soil factors. The eleventh factor is the genetic material of the plant itself, which we have limited control over and influences the specific plant's needs.

The five above-ground plant growth factors are:

- Light
- Temperature
- Humidity
- Airflow
- Carbon dioxide ($CO_2$) levels

The five in-soil plant growth factors are:

- Biodiversity
- Water
- Root health
- Nutrition
- Soil temperature

# ABOVE-GROUND PLANT GROWTH FACTORS

While we're going to explore the reasons and effects of these five factors separately, it should be noted that at some point, each element depends on other factors as part of the whole system.

## Factor 1: Light Levels

Below is a table of light units and their description, a reference of terms used in this section.

| TERM | DEFINITION |
|---|---|
| Daily Light Integral (DLI) ($mol \cdot m-2 \cdot d-1$) | The cumulative amount of photosynthetically active radiation (PAR) delivered each day expressed as moles of light (mol) per square meter ($m^{-2}$ (10.8 sq ft)) per day (d-1). |
| Foot-candle (fc) | Photometric unit based on visible light. Subject to some limitations. |
| Joules (J) | Unit for energy measuring the capacity to perform work or generate heat |
| Mole (mol) | A standard scientific unit for measuring large quantities of microscopic entities such as atoms, molecules, or photons. ($6.022 \times 10^{23}$). Also known as the Avogadro constant. ($6.022 \times 10^{23}$ mol-1) |
| Micromole (µmol) | A micromole represents one-millionth of a mole and is often denoted as µmol or umol. Given that a mole roughly equates to $6.022140857 \times 10^{23}$ entities, it means that: 1 µmol corresponds to $6.022140857 \times 10^{17}$ entities |
| Nanometer (nm) | A billionth of a meter ($1 \times 10^{-9}$ m). Used to measure wavelengths. |
| PAR Sensor | Instrument designed to measure photosynthetic photon flux density (PPFD) |
| Photon | A particle representing a quantum of light carrying energy proportional to the wavelength (color) |
| Photosynthetically Active Radiation (PAR) | Photons with wavelengths between 400 to 700 nm capable of stimulating photosynthesis. Radiation that drives photosynthesis. |
| Photon Flux Density | Number of photons that flow through a unit area per unit time, for example, $mol \cdot m-2 \cdot d-1$ or $µmol \cdot m-2 \cdot s-1$ |
| Photosynthetic Photon Flux Density (PPFD) | The amount of PAR reaching a unit area in a given time, for example, $µmol \cdot m-2 \cdot s-1$ or $mol \cdot m-2 \cdot d-1$. The photon flux density in the 400 to 700 nm wavelength range. |
| Photometric Unit (fc or lux) | The subjective measurement of perceived light brightness. 1 fc = 10.8 lux. Lux is a metric unit of illuminance equal to one lumen per square meter. |
| Quantum Unit ($µmol \cdot m-2 \cdot s-1$) | The number of PAR micromoles reaching a surface area of one square meter every second. Quantum meters are the most effective means of measuring PAR light intensity. |
| Ultraviolet Radiation (UV) | Wavelengths from 100 to 400 nm. An undamaged ozone layer should block harmful UV below 300 nm. |
| Watt (W) | A metric unit of power or radiant flux equal to 1 joule per second |

Plants are autotrophs (self-nourishing), using energy from light to produce organic molecules, mainly glucose. The efficiency of their glucose and fructose production depends on light quantity and quality, $CO_2$ availability, and water quality and availability. Plants get their daily energy from the glucose and fructose they produce and their long-term energy from the starches they store. Starch storage is usually in their roots and is used as a source of energy to emerge from dormancy when they have no leaves for photosynthesis. Daily energy availability is vital as it drives other processes that produce proteins, fats, and nucleic acids used as a defense network. In consuming the gained energy, plants respire, releasing $CO_2$ and water, a reverse of the photosynthesis process.

### Photosynthesis

Let's start with light because that's where the plant gets the energy for photosynthesis. Here are some characteristics of light and their effect on plant growth:

Light has a particulate nature, and those particles are called photons. Because photons are so small, they're measured in bundles called mole (mol) using the Avogadro constant, i.e., $6.022 \times 10^{23}$ photons per mole.

Light travels in waves, and the varying wavelengths result in different colors. Wavelengths are measured in nanometers, which is a billionth of a meter ($1 \times 10^{-9}$ m) or 0.000,000,001 m.

Human eyes are less capable than birds and bees, with human eyes only able to compute wavelengths between 390 and 750 nm. Birds and pollinators typically use ultraviolet light, which is below 390 nm. On the other hand, reptiles and amphibians use the longer infrared wavelength to find their prey, a light with a wavelength of more than 800 nm.

Because foot-candle (fc) measurements are based on subjective human sight, fc readings will vary significantly in measuring constant light from different light sources. Consider getting a PAR meter to measure photosynthetic photon flux density (PPFD) more accurately.

[top right] These luscious black grapes in the tunnel bask in warm sunlight. They have the perfect growing conditions that contribute to the development of these sweet and flavorful fruits.

### The Effects of Different Light Spectrums

Within the visible light spectrum, the longest wavelengths are red light. Longer wavelengths, invisible to the human eye, include infrared radiation. The shortest wavelengths visible to the human eye are blue and violet light; shorter wavelengths invisible to us include UV light.

Blue light affects plant growth, as does far red. I suggest you view the YouTube video "Photobiology Simplified with Dr. Bruce Bugbee" for a summary of some extensive research on the effects of light on plant growth and shape.

We're interested in the PPFD because PAR provides the energy that drives photosynthesis, synthesizing light energy into chemical energy. This light energy takes low-energy $CO_2$ and water ($H_2O$) and produces high-energy carbohydrates and oxygen ($CH_2O + O_2$). Plants are only 30 percent effective in conversion, and adverse conditions can drive that efficiency even lower. Photosynthesis consists of twenty-three steps, and a loss of only a few percentage points in each process results in a combined loss of 70 percent.

Photosynthesis takes $CO_2$ and $H_2O$ and produces something exponentially higher in energy—a carbohydrate, some oxygen, and heat. While we all marvel at the simplicity of Einstein's $e = mc^2$, the $CO_2 + H_2O = CH_2O + O_2$ is life's foundational formula, without which we would all cease to exist. The energy produced synthesizes monomers into amino acids, lipids, and nucleic acids during the night. During respiration, the photosynthesis-produced $CH_2O + O_2$ are converted into $CO_2$ and $H_2O$. The growth process is two steps forward and one step back, the cost of plant function, health, and resilience.

As far as our topic, light, is concerned, three principal characteristics affect plant growth, health, and resilience: quality, quantity, and duration.

### *Light Quality*

Light quality refers to the spectrum of visible and invisible colors that reach the plant's leaves. Plants respond most strongly to red and blue light, as both are used by plants in their food production. Vegetative (leaf) growth is predominantly triggered by blue light. When red lighting is added to blue light, blooming is promoted. Because foliage reflects green light rather than absorbing it, plants appear green.

For a more controlled crop, it's crucial to know how to manipulate the light quality. Fluorescent (cool white) light, for instance, has a large percentage of blue light, and it's perfect for germinating seeds and fostering the development of new leaves. While incandescent bulbs produce a lot of heat, they also emit a lot of light, making them less than ideal for use in a greenhouse. Grow lights offer a spectrum of red and blue light to simulate sunlight but aren't necessarily more effective. Variable bulbs that can be adjusted to give different light qualities at different growth phases are best but expensive.

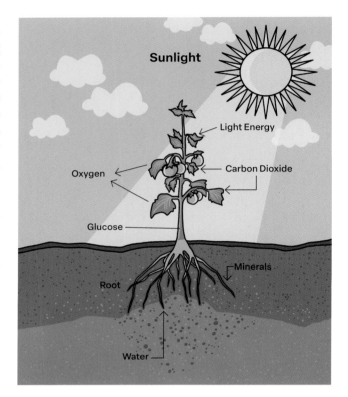

[top] Photosynthesis is a multistep process that is influenced by many factors.

[bottom] Here, I'm conducting a light levels experiment using a Spider Farmer® SF2000, assessing the reach and quality of light to optimize growing conditions and ensure the health and productivity of my plants.

## *Light Quantity*

Light quantity refers to the number of photons within the 400 to 700 nm range (PAR) present, with summer offering the most intense natural light, while winter is generally less severe. The amount of available light is calculated in micromoles per square meter per second, or mole per square meter per day ($\mu mol \cdot m-2 \cdot s-1$ or $mol \cdot m-2 \cdot d-1$). Of prime interest is the light quality (wavelength) and light quantity reaching a leaf surface (photosynthetic photon flux density [PPFD]), i.e., the photon flux density in the 400 to 700 nm wavelength range. Overly dense foliage or shade from taller plants can impact the PPFD value, as this is generally measured on the leaf surface.

The light intensity can be adjusted to influence how a plant develops, boosting available light by using reflective materials, a white background, or more lighting. Use woven shade cloths to block the sun's rays for plants that require less light. If you want to block out light totally, consider using black sateen cloth, a jet-black woven cotton/polyester material, or polyolefin sheeting, a tear-resistant and waterproof woven material.

Constructing a potting bench and incorporating mylar reflects light and enhances growing conditions. The light is notably bouncing off the mylar, illuminating my face as I work diligently on the project.

### *Photoperiodism*

A photoperiod is the duration of light within a twenty-four-hour cycle. A twelve-hour photoperiod consists of twelve hours of light and twelve hours of darkness, whereas a ten-hour photoperiod consists of ten hours of light and fourteen hours of darkness. Photoperiodism is the term for the responses of plants to photoperiods.

Some plants need a definite amount of darkness to flower. While it was long held that light is essential to plant health, it has now been shown that the duration of the absence of light is as vital for some plants. We now understand that the length of continuous darkness is more important for flower development in some plants than the length of the light period. In accordance with their sensitivity to changes in light and dark cycles, plants are divided into short-day (long-night), long-day (short-night), and day-neutral.

The day must be less than twelve hours for short-day plants to produce flowers. Several plants fit this description, including soybeans, poinsettias, and chrysanthemums. Poinsettias need a night of at least sixteen hours for three weeks before they will flower. Growers ensure this happens by using block-out materials, ensuring plants will be ready for the market over the festive season.

However, long-day plants only produce flowers when the length of a day is greater than twelve hours. Long-day vegetables include Swiss chard, beet, radish, lettuce, and spinach.

Day-neutral plants will bloom irrespective of the lengths of the nights. All the nightshade family (Solanaceae), corn, and cucumber plants are all day-neutral.

If you're particularly interested in manipulating plant growth (photosynthesis) and development (shape) using lights, check out the USDA-funded Lighting Approaches to Maximize Profits (LAMP) project.[44]

The striking colors of ruby chard growing in the garden—its vibrant hues and lush foliage showcase the beauty and appeal of this nutritious and versatile leafy green vegetable.

## Factor 2: Ambient Temperature

This section explores the role of temperatures in plant health and production and ways to manage temperatures in the immediate plant environment. Seed germination, photosynthesis, respiration, turgidity, dormancy, and fruiting are all affected by temperature.

### *Dormancy*

The dormant state is generally triggered by changing day length and temperature changes. Most plants are winter-dormant, but others (especially succulents) go dormant in summer. Others, such as the oxalis, have multiple dormant stages. Dormancy is an essential phase for perennials and biennials. Some plants won't flower unless the nights are longer than the days, and several of these also require some cold to trigger development. Though times vary, most trees won't sprout blossoms before being exposed to 700 and 1,000 hours in temperatures below 45°F (7.2°C).

In a state of dormancy, buds can withstand temperatures well below freezing, but once the plant has started emerging from dormancy, buds are far more susceptible to damage from late cold or frost. Temperatures well above average in the winter can cause some plants to break dormancy early, leaving them vulnerable to frost damage as temperatures drop.

Potatoes, for instance, should be planted in soil temperatures between 60°F and 70°F (15°C and 21°C) but not above 80°F (27°C). Tubers will not form if soil temperatures are too high. While a raised bed improves drainage, it also can cause soil temperatures to rise faster, so keep an eye on that.

Tomatoes perform better in high temperature stress (HTS) environments if seedlings are given ten minutes daily cold-shock therapy at 50°F (10°C). These short cold spells trigger an adaptive response that improves plant stress resistance.[45]

Plant seed potatoes when soil temperatures are just right—between 60°F and 70°F (15°C and 21°C).

### *Photosynthesis and Respiration*

A rise in temperature typically results in an increase in photosynthesis and transpiration rates. Most plants photosynthesize most efficiently between 65°F and 85°F (~18°C to 29°C), with nighttime temperatures above 50°F (10°C). Therefore, plants enjoy the most productive thermoperiod when day temperatures are 10°F to 15°F (5°C to 8°C) higher than night temperatures. These temperatures are optimal for daytime photosynthesis and transpiration, suppressing some nighttime respiration (food breakdown). Note though that over suppression of transpiration can compromise the plant's resilience which is strengthened by the presence of amino acids, lipids, and nucleic acids.

### *Plant Productivity*

If temperatures are high and the day length is long, cool-season crops can blossom early (bolt) rather than grow the essential leaves we want to harvest. Many vegetables cultivated as annuals are biennials, but we harvest them in their first year. These include root vegetables such as beets, turnips, carrots, parsnips, rutabaga, onions, leeks, and shallots. (Note: shallots won't form a good bulb once it flowers.) Biennial leafy vegetables such as kale, endive, Swiss chard, and collards are prone to bolting. Other plants that can bolt are Brussels sprouts, cauliflower, celery, cabbage, kohlrabi, and parsley. Extreme temperature fluctuations can cause stunted growth and poor quality. Bolted plants such as lettuce and cucumbers become unpalatable. High temperatures can impact pollen-count, preventing fruit set. Conversely, low temperatures can inhibit fruit set in warm-season crops such as tomatoes.

These multisown beets are thriving in the garden, accompanied by a reminder of the importance of monitoring light and temperature conditions to prevent bolting and ensure a successful, bountiful harvest.

### Water Consumption

In hot temperatures, plants lose water faster than they can absorb it, causing wilting and inhibiting growth. Extremely cold temperatures can cause the soil to freeze, reducing the bioavailable water. A combination of high temperatures and wind can rapidly dehydrate as transpiration rates increase beyond the plant's ability to replenish foliar water availability. Frost blackened plants are caused by burst plant cells created when the water in the plant expands as it freezes, destroying cells.

### Temperature Management

*Cloche* is the French word for bell, and gardening cloches used to look like pastry displays. The term has been adopted to represent anything that can cover a plant or two, even being used for solid transparent row covers. Rather than trying to cover (spot the pun) all the possible varieties of cloches, let's explore the principles:

- Cloches can be made of mesh to protect plants from nibblers that might want to snack on seedlings.

- Closed cloches allow you to create a terrarium of sorts, limiting airflow and trapping heat and water vapor. They often are used to lengthen the growing season, allowing you to protect your plant from adverse environmental risks.

- Closed cloches absorb solar radiation and prevent soil and plant moisture from evaporating.

- Cloches are light, portable, and re-usable. A cloche can be made of fleece, plastic, mesh, glass, or recycled PET plastic containers—the choice is yours.

- I use them mainly at night to minimize frost damage and remove them during the day to allow air circulation.

- Cloches should be tethered or heavy enough to prevent them from blowing away.

[top right] Netting brassica beds effectively safeguards the plants from damage by birds and frost, emphasizing the importance of implementing protective measures for a healthy, uninterrupted growing season.

Row covers and low tunnels with fabric or plastic can be pulled over half-hoops and sealed around the borders to trap heat, exclude pests, and limit wind. Plastic mulch and drip irrigation are frequently paired with covers and low tunnels. The sole difference between these two methods is that the low tunnel system uses wire hoops to hold up the material above the plants. Both closed cloches and row covers can boost temperatures by 5°F to 6°F (~3°C) while also screening out pests easily, resulting in extended seasons and improved quality crops.

Ensure that you keep a close eye on your plants and their environment to avoid trapping pests inside of coverings, excluding pollinators, and over-heating plants. If the temperature under the cover exceeds 90°F (32°C) for several hours, Solanaceae family crops will suffer (see page 168). Ideally, row covers should have a way to be rolled up to boost ventilation when temperatures get too high. Vegetables from the Cucurbitaceae family (see page 144) are more heat resistant.

Cold frames and hotbeds are basic, low-cost structures that provide a conducive climate for producing cool-weather crops in the early spring, fall, and winter months. Some are elaborate and demand a significant investment, but the majority are reasonably priced for people who want to extend their growing season.

If you want to extend your growing season further, convert your cold frame to a hotbed by adding an additional heating system, either underbed manure composting or underfloor waterproof electrical heating mats. Decomposing manure compost generates temperatures of up to 160°F (71°C), but if unturned and left in situ would average around 70°F (21°C). Heating mats generally run at 77°F (25°C), the optimal seed germination temperature.

Cold frames and hotbeds can be used to:

- Increase the length of growing season by starting plants earlier and providing protection for plants in the fall.

- Overwinter semihardy plants.

- Start transplants.

Cold frames and hotbeds must be monitored to prevent extreme heat, intense sunlight, and overwatering. Damage can be avoided by using shade cloth to shade the windows when required. Also, because the virtually airtight cold frame reduces evaporation, it is easy to overwater. Water early in the day, allowing plants to dry before dark to help avoid fungal infestations.

## Extend Your Growing Season

Try these to create a healthy climate for growing year round.

- Cold frame: A solid, angled construction with a glass door or window covering over the top.

- Hotbed: Similar to a cold frame, but with a supplemental heat source which could be organic such as manure or compost, or nonorganic, such as heating mats.

Built at a slight south-facing angle, cold frames capture UV light to warm the interior, heating the soil and environment. Temperature regulation and pollinator access is made possible by opening and ventilating the cold frame, and you can avoid unnecessary opening and closing by incorporating a drip irrigation system. There are several YouTube videos that show how to use old window frames to build your own cold frame or hotbed.

These large cold frames are ingeniously built on the back of the shed in the well-being garden of Simplify Gardening, exemplifying the resourceful integration of garden structures to nurture tender plants and seedlings.

### *Polytunnels*

Polytunnels, or hoop houses, are made of PVC or metal bows that are attached to metal posts driven into the ground. The bows are covered in one to two layers of greenhouse-grade polyethylene, high enough to walk under. Tunnels are ventilated by manually rolling up the sides in the morning and down in the evening. High tunnels are a good middle ground between unheated low tunnels and heated greenhouses. They improve crop growth, yield, and quality, and although they provide some frost protection, their major role is to raise temperatures by a few degrees per day for several weeks. By using row covers inside polytunnels, plants can be afforded even higher temperature gains.

Here is lush and vibrant growth within the new polytunnel at Simplify Gardening. The controlled environment fosters a wide variety of flourishing plants and vegetables.

The homemade polytunnel in Simplify Gardening's garden, skillfully repurposed as a propagation area to nurture seedlings and cuttings, highlights the adaptability and resourcefulness of gardeners in optimizing our spaces.

## Factor 3: Humidity

Humidity is the amount of water vapor in the air. Absolute humidity is the water vapor an air volume can hold, generally expressed in grams per cubic meter. Relative humidity is the amount of water vapor as a percentage of the maximum amount the air can store at a given temperature.

### *Humidity Levels*

Humidity affects plant growth in various ways, depending on the type and stage of the plant, as well as the environmental conditions. Generally speaking, plants need some humidity to make photosynthesis possible and to prevent excessive water loss through transpiration. However, too much humidity can adversely affect plant health and productivity.

One of the factors that influence humidity is air temperature. Warm air can hold more water vapor than cold air, so when the temperature rises, the relative humidity decreases. Plants may experience different humidity levels throughout the day and night.

Low humidity can cause plants to close their stomata (tiny pores on their leaves) to conserve water, reducing their ability to take up carbon dioxide and release oxygen for photosynthesis. Low humidity can increase transpiration rates (water loss through evaporation), leading to wilting or drought stress.

High humidity can cause plants to open their stomata more often or for extended periods, increasing their gas exchange and photosynthesis rates. However, high humidity can reduce evaporation rates and create a humid microclimate around plant leaves, promoting the spread of fungal or bacterial diseases that damage plant tissues or reduce crop yields.

Optimal humidity levels vary depending on plant species and growing conditions. Some plants are adapted to dry environments (such as cacti or succulents), while others prefer moist environments (such as ferns or orchids). Some plants may benefit from higher humidity during certain stages of growth (such as seedlings or cuttings), while others may need lower humidity during flowering or fruiting stages.

An optimal relative humidity level for most plants is around 65 percent, which varies depending on plant species, light intensity, ventilation, or irrigation methods.

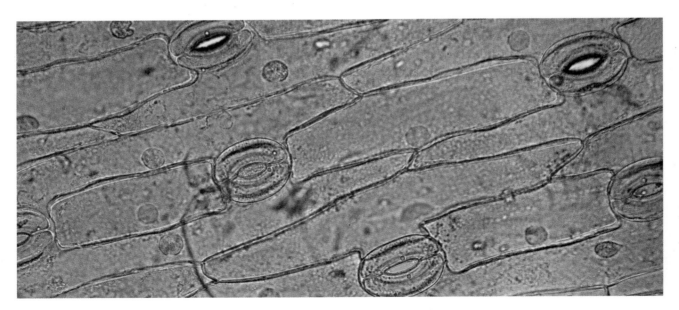

Stomata are small holes in plant leaves through which water vapor passes. Low humidity can cause stomata to close to conserve water, which also reduces carbon dioxide uptake and reduces photosynthesis.

| Absolute Humidity (Air's water-holding capacity at different temperatures) | |
| --- | --- |
| Temperature | Ounces/Cubic Yard (g/m³) |
| 122°F (50°C) | 2.24 (83.0) |
| 104°F (40°C) | 1.38 (51.1) |
| 86°F (30°C) | 0.82 (30.4) |
| 68°F (20°C) | 0.47 (17.3) |
| 50°F (10°C) | 0.25 (9.4) |
| 32°F (0°C) | 0.13 (4.8) |
| 14°F (-10°C) | 0.062 (2.3) |
| -4°F (-20°C) | 0.024 (0.9) |

### *Relative Humidity (RH)*

RH is the comparative percentage of actual water vapor in the air compared to its full capacity at a given temperature and air pressure. Let's say the temperature is 68°F (20°C), and the absolute humidity is 6.7 g/m³, then the RH would be 50 percent as the air only holds half of what it could hold at the same temperature.[46]

### *How Air Temperature Affects Humidity*

Humidity is the amount of water vapor in the air. The air's capacity to hold water vapor depends on its temperature. The warmer the air, the more water vapor it can contain; the cooler the air, the less water vapor it can hold.

Humidity changes when the temperature of the air changes. For instance, when warm air becomes cooler, it may reach its saturation point, the temperature at which the air cannot hold any more water vapor. At this point, some water vapor will turn into liquid water droplets, creating clouds or fog. Conversely, when cool air becomes warmer, it can contain more water vapor without being saturated, so its relative humidity will drop.

Humidity influences weather and climate in different ways. High humidity can make hot weather feel more stifling and unpleasant because sweat does not evaporate quickly from the skin. High humidity also raises the likelihood of precipitation and thunderstorms. Low humidity can make cold weather feel dry and harsh because moisture evaporates quickly from exposed surfaces. Low humidity also lowers cloud formation and rainfall.

Much of the water taken up by plants transpires, so a constant supply is necessary in order to prevent wilting.

## *Plant Transpiration*

Through transpiration, plants move water and nutrients from their roots to their stems and leaves. As the water travels through the leaves, it is released into the atmosphere through tiny pores (stomata). Interestingly, this process does not occur in succulent species that have evolved to keep their stomata closed during hot days and only breathe at night, limiting moisture loss.[47]

High humidity slows transpiration and, in effect, reduces water flow via the xylem (upward flow of water from the roots to leaves) while maintaining phloem activity—the downwards movement of photosynthesis-produced sugars throughout the plant. Remember that as much as 90 percent of the water given to plants transpires, ensuring a constant flow of fresh water through plants. An additional portion is lost in respiration, the product of biochemical processes responsible for synthesizing monomers into proteins, lipids, and amino acids.

## *Balancing Humidity and Airflow*

Balancing humidity and airflow is essential for keeping vegetable plants hydrated and healthy. Humidity affects how much water plants lose through transpiration, which affects their water uptake and nutrient transport. Airflow can help increase transpiration and gas exchange by disrupting the layer of air around plant leaves. However, plants can suffer from too much humidity and airflow.

High humidity can reduce water loss, cause lettuce to lack calcium, and increase fungal infections. The ideal humidity range for most vegetable crops is 50 to 70 percent. Depending on the situation, growers can use humidifiers, misters, fans, vents, or heaters to adjust the humidity if they grow indoors.

## Factor 4: Airflow

Though not often considered, airflow is a vital factor of plant health and development. As leaves transpire, they create a gaseous cocoon around themselves. Unlike humans that exhale at a rate that allows each successive breath to exclude much of the pervious exhalation, plants rely on air movement to remove their transpiration, especially when relative humidity levels are high.[48]

Airflow also ensures a better distribution of hot and cold air. Cold air is denser and therefore heavier than warm air. At night, every vertical 3 feet (91 cm) can have a temperature difference of 1.7°F. In other words, if the air above the ground is 55°F (12.8°C), then the air 3 feet (91 cm) above that would be 56.7°F (13.7°C). Airflow ensures a more uniform distribution of hot air around plants at night.

When plants are planted too close to each other, light and airflow is compromised and can impede plant growth. Insufficient airflow compromises evaporation rates and the growing dampness can promote the spread of fungi and their associated diseases.

### *Boundary Layer*

The humidity boundary layer around plant leaves is a thin layer of air that surrounds the leaf surface and has a different water vapor concentration than the ambient air. The humidity boundary layer affects the rate of transpiration, which is the loss of water from the leaf through the stomata (tiny pores).

The thickness and resistance of the humidity boundary layer depend on several factors, such as leaf size and shape, wind speed and direction, temperature, and humidity. A thicker and more resistant humidity boundary layer reduces the water vapor gradient between the leaf and the atmosphere, thus slowing down transpiration. A thinner and less resistant humidity boundary layer increases the water vapor gradient and enhances transpiration. Therefore, understanding and manipulating the humidity boundary layer can help optimize plant water use efficiency and productivity.

The cutout windows with mesh along the polytunnel are designed to provide optimal airflow during warmer months. A roll-down curtain also is featured for winter growing, highlighting the practical and adaptable nature of the structure.

Winds can quickly dry out soils and plants, causing more moisture to be lost through transpiration.

### *Temperature Management*

As mentioned earlier, cold air drops, flowing to the lowest places in your garden. Hot air rises, creating a vacuum that pulls the colder air in. This is most noticeable in greenhouses where the plants on the edges are slower at flowering than those in the center. Vertical airflow helps dissipate the colder air, forcing warmer air to mix in, improving overall temperature ranges. The speed of the airflow only needs to be 50 to 100 feet a minute (15 to 30 meters). Outdoors, that would equate to 0.5 to 1 mile per hour, or 0.8 to 1.6 km/h. Faster winds decimate boundary layers, increase plant drying, and could stress plants if wind is hot and dry. Cold winds can cause temperatures to drop fast. In windy areas, consider planting hedges to divert or slow wind speeds in the region of your garden without creating shade.

## Factor 5: $CO_2$ Levels

As we saw earlier, the Earth's atmosphere is (thankfully) only 0.04 percent carbon dioxide: a little more and we fry in a UV oven; too little and day-night extremes would be unbearable. We are truly thankful to nature for $CO_2$. Without $CO_2$ plants would not be able to produce their food.

The combustion of fossil fuels (including coal, oil, and natural gas), the burning of forests, and natural processes such as volcanic eruptions all contribute to the release of carbon dioxide ($CO_2$), an important heat-trapping gas. Human activities have increased atmospheric $CO_2$ by 50 percent since the beginning of industrial times (in the eighteenth century), bringing the current value to 150 percent of what it was in 1750. This exceeds the natural peak that occurred during the end of the last ice age, some 20,000 years ago.

In 2002 atmospheric $CO_2$ levels were 365 parts per million (ppm), in 2015, 400, and at the time of this writing, we have an apocalyptic 419 ppm.[49] These readings are from the mid-troposphere, the layer of Earth's atmosphere located between 6 to 7 miles (10 to 11 km) above sea level.

### Soil's Supply of $CO_2$

As the soil biome break organic material down, they're feeding on carbon and nitrogen, releasing $CO_2$ and water. The level of bioavailable nitrogen depends on having most of the organic material in your soil partially decomposed, which is the reason why adding compost to your soil is better than adding uncomposted organic material. If you add, say, uncomposted woodchips to your soil, the microorganisms will start breaking it down, but they require nitrogen to do that, causing the nitrogen available to your plants to drop.

Insects such as the fungus gnat determine the quality of a potential egg-laying site by the amount of $CO_2$ the soil releases. Because their larvae feed on fungi, and $CO_2$ are a good indicator of fungus activity, they know that soils releasing high levels of $CO_2$ are a great egg-laying option. It's one of the reasons gnats seem to insist on flying into your face; they're triggered by the $CO_2$ you exhale.

Here I am in action, filling a wheelbarrow with nutrient-rich homemade compost from a large pile, ready to be spread across the garden beds to nourish and enrich the soil for a bountiful growing season.

## IN-SOIL PLANT GROWTH FACTORS

### Factor 1: Biodiversity

Microorganisms consume carbon-rich material, often called brown materials, and nitrogen-rich green materials. Active microbes can be grouped as fungi, bacteria, and actinomycetes (a group with fungi and bacteria characteristics), and they are responsible for decomposing organic matter. Actinomycetes also are responsible for that lovely earthy smell of healthy soil, known as petrichor, primarily made up of an organic compound called geosmin.

The bacteria, fungi, and actinomycetes get their energy from carbon and use nitrogen for cellular growth. Protozoa, mites, nematodes, centipedes, and spiders, prey on these primary feeders, and in the process, nitrogen is released into the soil. The soil food web extends through the food chain, and at the top of the pyramid the macrofauna, the soil engineers (earthworms and ants) are eaten by birds, moles, and larger predators.

### *The Benefits of Soil Biodiversity*

It is commonly advised that compost is an alternative to fertilizer, but that's not quite true. The value of compost is not in its chemical composition, but rather the abundance and diversity of the microorganisms composting promotes. The key to nutritional soil is following the advice of soil tests and starting with soil that has balanced proportions of the required chemical elements.

Microorganisms are the most effective nutrient mobilizers, making the essential chemical elements bioavailable. Once the chemistry is balanced, soil biology ensures healthy water and air movement, escalated cation exchange capacity (CEC), and chemical compounds converted into plant absorbable monomers.

Healthy soil produces healthy plants, which in turn benefit people's health. Vegetables grown in healthy soil, with diverse micro- and macro-organisms, have improved pathogen defense systems and nutrition and offer better taste experiences.

**The Soil Food Web**

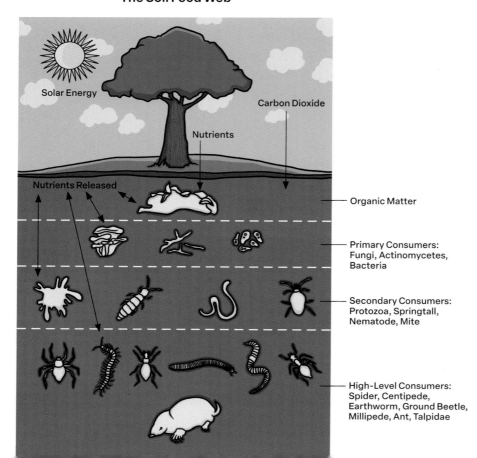

Solar Energy

Carbon Dioxide

Nutrients

Nutrients Released

Organic Matter

Primary Consumers: Fungi, Actinomycetes, Bacteria

Secondary Consumers: Protozoa, Springtall, Nematode, Mite

High-Level Consumers: Spider, Centipede, Earthworm, Ground Beetle, Millipede, Ant, Talpidae

[left] The soil food web, and its extensive cast of characters, is key to fostering a healthy, productive vegetable garden.

[page right, left] My composting bay is filled with dark, nutrient-dense compost, matured and ready to be harvested, underscoring the vital role that compost plays in nurturing healthy, productive gardens.

[page right, right] Plants are composed primarily of water, so ensuring your plants have an adequate supply translates to optimum plant performance.

## Factor 2: Water Supply

Water serves many critical functions in all living organisms. In plants, water plays a pivotal role in photosynthesis and serves as a transport vehicle for mineral salts (ions) and carbohydrates.[50]

### *Water's Roles in Plant Growth*

Water is essential to plant growth and health. Below is a list of some of water's functions in plant growth and health:

- Water as a constituent: As much as 80 to 90 percent of the fresh weight of plants is water.

- Water as a solvent: Water serves as the medium in which biological reactants are dissolved in cells for chemical reactions.

- Water as a reactant: In the biochemical reactions of the cell, water is a reactant. One of these processes is photosynthesis, where water provides hydrogen protons necessary for producing adenosine triphosphate (ATP) and electrons ultimately used to reduce carbon to a carbohydrate. Water also contributes to the oxygen that is produced during photosynthesis.

- Water as essential transport: Water circulation carries the minerals from the soil across the root, up the stem, and throughout the plant. Carbohydrates, which develop in photosynthesis, also are distributed through the plant by water.

- Water as a component of growth: Small cavities (vacuoles) form during cell division, absorbing water that transports mineral deposits. As the water diffuses into the tiny vacuoles, it creates pressure inside the cell, causing them to expand and increase. As the cells mature, they no longer grow but maintain water pressure inside as the vacuoles merge and unite into a central vacuole. The walls get so thick that they lose elasticity.

- Water and turgidity: Water pressure against mature cells' interior helps keep their form. If the pressure is lost (for example, due to excessive evaporation, fungal infections, or exposure to salt solutions), the cells may lose their turgidity and become flaccid (wilt).

- Water and the plant's thermal stability: Water requires more heat energy to raise its temperature than other common substances. Because of this, plants, composed primarily of water, may absorb a large quantity of heat (such as from sunshine) while slowly increasing in temperature. Similarly, the same number of calories must be wasted to drop the water temperature (for a plant), allowing the plant temperature to stay close to air temperature during brief cold spells. The high-water content in a plant helps aid temperature stability while air temperatures fluctuate.

### Water Management

Generally, vegetables need between an 1 to 1.5 inches (2.5 to 4 cm) of water per week, depending on the vegetable crop, development stage, current soil moisture levels, soil type, and weather conditions. A 40-square foot vegetable bed (10 × 4 ft) needs 25 to 37.5 gallons of water per week. In metric units, a bed that is 3 meters by 120 centimeters will need between 91.5 liters and 137 liters of water per week. We explore water management in more detail in the next section.

### Water Risks

Some of the risks of using urban water sources for vegetable garden irrigation are:

**Contamination:** Urban water sources may contain harmful chemicals that can affect the quality and safety of the vegetables. Some plants are sensitive to chlorine and fluoride; they will benefit from you keeping the water in a bucket overnight, allowing these volatile chemicals to evaporate.

**Salinity:** Urban water sources may have high salt levels due to seawater intrusion, road salt, or water softeners. Excess salt can damage the plant cells and roots, reduce nutrient uptake, and cause wilting, browning, or stunted growth. Salt can increase soil pH and affect soil fertility and microbial activity.

**Alkalinity:** Urban water sources may have high pH levels due to lime or concrete leaching into the water. High pH can reduce the availability of essential nutrients such as iron, manganese, and zinc, and it can cause chlorosis (yellowing) or necrosis (browning) of the leaves. High pH can affect soil structure and drainage.

**Pressure:** Urban water sources may have high pressure due to pumps or valves that regulate the flow of water. High pressure can cause erosion of the soil surface, compaction of the soil layers, and loss of organic matter. High pressure also can damage the plant stems and leaves by causing breakage or bruising.

Before using it for vegetable garden irrigation, avoid these risks by testing the water source for its quality parameters such as pH, salinity, hardness, and contaminants. Consider using appropriate irrigation methods

Four IBCs have been ingeniously set up to collect rainwater from my polytunnel and shed, serving as an environmentally friendly irrigation system to provide plants with a natural water source while conserving valuable resources.

such as drip irrigation or soaker hoses that deliver water directly to the plant roots and minimize evaporation and runoff. Additionally, monitoring the soil moisture level regularly and adjusting the watering frequency to prevent overwatering or underwatering.

## Factor 3: Root Health

The rhizosphere's, or root zone's, functionality is arguably the most critical to plant health and resilience. Here the plant accesses water, exchanges gases, and uses varied mechanisms to access nutrients. The rhizosphere also serves as the main area where the plant actively interacts with a diverse soil biome, including bacteria, fungi, actinomycetes, nematodes, arthropods, and others. Several fungal diseases originate from the rhizosphere, but so too does plant antibody production.

### Breathing Roots

Initially, NASA scientists thought plants purify air via their leaves due to photosynthesis and respiration functions.[51] It has now been discovered that most of that purification is performed by plant roots, even in the absence of any foliage.[52] The German-based AIRY GreenTech has used these finding (now in the public domain) to develop a pot to optimize plant purification functions indoors.

### Soil Water Management Capacities

A plant's access to water depends on the growing medium's ability to manage available hydration, a contest between capillary action, evaporation, gravity, and cation exchange capacity (CEC). The song by The Clash "Should I Stay or Should I Go" comes to mind, or Leonard Cohen's "Passing Through"—or maybe Jeremy Camp's "Consumed."

Soil receives water from rain or irrigation and loses it through drainage, evaporation, and transpiration. Variation in the pore space of soil affects its ability to store water. Soils containing equal parts air and water in their pores are ideal. Plants will die if their roots are exposed to too much air, and anaerobic conditions (the absence of air) causes a loss of plant vitality and root rot becomes more likely.

## Saturation Porosity

We're interested in the soil's ability to absorb water without sacrificing the air in the soil, known as the *saturation porosity*. A quality soil allows the water to drain through it, keeping some water without compromising the availability of air.[53] The difference between added and drained water amounts to the water retained in the soil, and is the field capacity. Complimenting field capacity is saturation porosity, the air content remaining in the soil after saturation and drainage.[54]

The health of your soil directly translates to the health of your plant and its roots. Quality soil absorbs water and holds it while still letting excess water drain away.

Soil aggregation determines the pore sizes of a soil and how readily
water moves through it. Aggregates such as these are formed by
the organic matter that "glues" the soil particles together.

The number of macropores (large), mesopores (medium), and micropores (small) in soils vary according to soil structure and soil biota activity. Sandier soils tend to have more macropores, which can quickly absorb water and drain it away. Drainage speed also is influenced by the presence of adhesion and cohesion forces contenting with gravity. In the presence of CEC, a product of carbon particle size, water can resist gravitation forces, increasing its availability to plants.

While mesopores hold more water, they are the first to dry up as water is lost to root uptake and transpiration. Micropores may still contain water, but this is stored so tightly that it is not accessible to plants. If a plant loses water via its leaves quicker than it can absorb it through its roots, it may wilt temporarily before reaching the permanent wilting point. An adequate water supply, loam soil (balancing meso- and micropores), and a high CEC (ample compost rich in biodiversity) is needed to ensure plants can maintain a healthy balance between uptake and transpiration, allowing them to recover from wilting during the day and flourish once the sun sets.

## Factor 4: Bioavailable Nutrition

Plants need a wide range of chemical elements for healthy growth and productivity and have interesting ways of getting access to them. I realize we have long been conditioned to believe NPK fertilizer is the source of plant vitality. However, there's growing evidence showing that, rather than plants being passive autotrophs (self-feeders), they have well developed strategies to recruit microorganisms to bring them the nutrients they need. Also, these nutrients are widely available in almost all soils, sans additions.

Regrettably, our popular NPK fertilizer strategy interrupts these processes, self-perpetuating a cycle of chemical dependence. The best possible strategy for improving plant nutrient availability is to boost soil biodiverse populations, both of plant roots and microorganisms. There is a strong link between plant family diversity and microbial diversity.

Effective diversity happens when plants from at least four families grow together with different germination times and root structures. The long-term study by the German Jena Experiment[55] has conclusively shown that environments become more effective and resilient if at least four species from four families, i.e., sixteen or more plants, are grown together.[56]

The evolution of agriculture in the world's rich, developed countries has four defining eras:

- Settled Agriculture
- Mechanical, and
- High Effort
- Chemical

Forced by growing food inequality and the accompanying societal pressures, rising input costs, and declining profits, agriculture is hard-pressed to find alternatives. Gone are the yield records for nine major U.S. crops during the twentieth century. The predicted 3 percent yield growth per annum did not materialize, despite bioengineered seeds and copious amounts of fertilizer. The last decade has seen an average annual NPK use of almost 215 million tons (195 million tonnes), of which 186 million tons (169 million tonnes) is nitrogen.[57]

The negative effects of nitrogen addition on soil microbial population size and diversity increase with nitrogen volumes and exposure time. High phosphate reduces arbuscular mycorrhizal symbiosis and the endophytes in seeds are nullified if planted in fertilized soil. We explore plant nutrition in more detail in chapter 5.

This truss of large tomatoes is just beginning to show hints of color as they gradually ripen on the vine, showcasing the remarkable transformation from green to red and the promise of a bountiful harvest.

## Factor 5: Soil Temperature

Temperature plays an important part in plant growth, both ambient temperature and soil temperature. Soil temperatures are essential for seed germination activity and even harvesting for root crops. First, let's consider how soil temperature affects planting times.

### *Vegetable Planting Timing*

Three factors influence plant timing:

- Soil temperatures

- The number of days to maturity

- The expected first frost date

## Root Vegetable Soil Temperatures

Parsnip grows best in cool weather; it prefers temperatures between 60°F and 65°F (16°C and 18°C). It also requires plenty of moisture and organic matter. Raised beds are ideal for producing parsnips, but you can use containers.

The roots become sweeter after a light frost when the starch converts to sugars, which happens when the plant tips freeze. You should harvest them before the ground freezes or protect them from freezing with a cover. To harvest a parsnip, you must dig around the plant area to expose the top of the root. Then you must pull it from the ground by holding it just above the base.

[top] When to plant transplants and seeds in your garden depends on what you're planting, the soil temperature, and more.

[bottom] The healthy growth of parsnips at Simplify Gardening. Their lush foliage stands tall as an indication of the thriving root vegetables hidden below the soil, eagerly awaiting harvest time.

Below is a list of cool- and warm-season crops and their respective germination temperature ranges and seed-to-harvest averages, allowing you to calculate each crop's best time to plant. Several crops that can be transplanted are cultivated indoors, allowing you to buy some time while the last frost passes. The list is ordered according to hardiness, starting with the most cold-hardy plants. Remember that the given temperatures refer to soil temperatures.

## Vegetables Ordered by Hardiness

| Plant | Growth Season | Ideal Soil Temperature | Germination Range | Planting | Seed-to-Harvest (Days) |
|-------|--------------|------------------------|-------------------|----------|------------------------|
| Spinach | Cool | 50°F (10°C) | 40°F–75°F (~4°C–24°C) | Direct | 45 |
| Broccoli | Cool | 77°F (25°C) | 45°F–85°F (~7°C–30°C) | Transplant | 110 |
| Brussels Sprouts | Cool | 77°F (25°C) | 45°F–85°F (~7°C–30°C) | Transplant | 85 |
| Cabbage | Cool | 77°F (25°C) | 45°F–85°F (~7°C–30°C) | Transplant | 85 |
| Cauliflower | Cool | 77°F (25°C) | 45°F–85°F (~7°C–30°C) | Transplant | 85 |
| Collard Greens | Cool | 77°F (25°C) | 45°F–85°F (~7°C–30°C) | Direct | 50 |
| Endive | Cool | 75°F (24°C) | 45°F–85°F (~7°C–30°C) | Direct | 90 |
| Kale | Cool | 60°F (16°C) | 45°F–85°F (~7°C–30°C) | Direct | 85 |
| Kohlrabi | Cool | 77°F (25°C) | 45°F–85°F (~7°C–30°C) | Direct | 45 |
| Lettuce | Cool | 70°F (21°C) | 45°F–85°F (~7°C–30°C) | Direct | 60 |
| Mustard | Cool | 60°F (16°C) | 45°F–85°F (~7°C–30°C) | Direct | 45 |
| Onions | Cool | 72°F (22°C) | 45°F–85°F (~7°C–30°C) | Direct | Varies |
| Rutabaga | Cool | 60°F (16°C) | 45°F–85°F (~7°C–30°C) | Direct | 90 |
| Turnip | Cool | 60°F (16°C) | 45°F–85°F (~7°C–30°C) | Direct | 45 |
| Scallions | Cool | 72°F (22°C) | 45°F–95°F (~7°C–30°C) | Direct | Varies |
| Shallots | Cool | 72°F (22°C) | 45°F–95°F (~7°C–30°C) | Direct | Varies |
| Chives | Cool | 77°F (25°C) | 45°F–95°F (~7°C–35°C) | Direct | Perennial |
| Leeks | Cool | 77°F (25°C) | 45°F–95°F (~7°C–35°C) | Transplant | 90 |

(continued on page 84)

| | | Vegetables Ordered by Hardiness | | | |
|---|---|---|---|---|---|
| Plant | Growth Season | Ideal Soil Temperature | Germination Range | Planting | Seed-to-Harvest (Days) |
| Bok Choy | Cool | 65°F (18°C) | 50°F–80°F (-10°C–27°C) | Transplant | 50 |
| Beets | Cool | 70°F (21°C) | 50°F–85°F (-10°C–30°C) | Direct | 60 |
| Carrots | Cool | 80°F (27°C) | 50°F–85°F (-10°C–30°C) | Direct | 75 |
| Parsnip | Cool | 77°F (25°C) | 50°F–85°F (-10°C–30°C) | Direct | 120 |
| Swiss Chard | Cool | 85°F (29°C) | 50°F–85°F (-10°C–30°C) | Direct | 60 |
| Radishes | Cool | 77°F (25°C) | 55°F–85°F (-13°C–30°C) | Direct | 42 |
| Celery | Cool | 72°F (22°C) | 70°F–75°F (~21°C–24°C) | Transplant | 80 |
| Potato | Warm | 75°F (24°C) | 42°F–95°F (~6°C–35°C) | Direct | 100 |
| Peas | Warm | 75°F (24°C) | 60°F–85°F (-16°C–30°C) | Direct | 60 |
| Cucumber | Warm | 85°F (29°C) | 60°F–90°F (-16°C–32°C) | Direct | 55 |
| Eggplant | Warm | 85°F (29°C) | 60°F–95°F (-16°C–35°C) | Transplant | 84 |
| Gourds | Warm | 85°F (29°C) | 60°F–95°F (-16°C–35°C) | Direct | 140 |
| Melons | Warm | 85°F (29°C) | 60°F–95°F (-16°C–35°C) | Direct | 80 |
| Pumpkin | Warm | 85°F (29°C) | 60°F–95°F (-16°C–35°C) | Direct | 75 |
| Squash | Warm | 85°F (29°C) | 60°F–95°F (-16°C–35°C) | Direct | 60 |
| Tomato | Warm | 82°F (28°C) | 60°F–95°F (-16°C–35°C) | Transplant | 75 |
| Corn–Sweet | Warm | 77°F (25°C) | 65°F–85°F (-18°C–30°C) | Direct | 75 |
| Beans | Warm | 77°F (25°C) | 70°F–80°F (-21°C–27°C) | Direct | 60 |
| Lima Beans | Warm | 77°F (25°C) | 70°F–80°F (-21°C–27°C) | Direct | 65 |
| Soybean | Warm | 77°F (25°C) | 70°F–80°F (-21°C–27°C) | Direct | 85 |
| Peppers | Warm | 85°F (29°C) | 70°F–95°F (-21°C–35°C) | Transplant | 80 |
| Watermelon | Warm | 85°F (29°C) | 70°F–95°F (-21°C–35°C) | Direct | 90 |

### *Managing Soil Temperature*

Following are some techniques you can use to raise soil temperatures:

- Cold frame or hotbox (see page 68)

- Raised beds (see page 52)

- Mulch—as a form of insulation

- Solarization—the use of dark materials to absorb the full spectrum of light, concentrating it to warm the soil

- Transparent cover—the use of materials to allow UV rays to penetrate, but blocking the heat from escaping

- Water evaporation—cools the soil as the water absorbs surrounding energy

Now that we've examined the factors that affect plant health, let's look at some ways we can influence them to optimize the health and production of our vegetable plants.

When you focus on both above-ground and in-ground plant growth factors, the results are beautiful and delicious.

A promising image featuring recently planted endive starts nestled within a polytunnel, capturing the anticipation and potential of these tender greens as they begin their journey toward full growth and harvest.

# Chapter 4:
## Optimizing Plant Health

We've looked at Earth's different macrosystems, how they interrelate, and how each impacts the way we grow food. In the previous chapter, we explored the eleven plant growth factors. This chapter explores the plant microsystems responsible for plant health to realize optimal food production.

### PROPAGATION

One of nature's wonders is that a whole plant and future generations of that plant can be encapsulated in a single seed. But getting seeds (and fruit) requires male and female participation. Some plants have flowers with male and female organs in a single flower. These are called perfect flowers, and the flowers from most commercial tomatoes are perfect (hermaphroditic). Other plants, such as the pumpkin, have monoecious flowers, meaning there are separate male and some female flowers on the same plant. A third group, such as asparagus and radish, is dioecious, with separate male and female plants. Reproduction of plants can be from seeds, a product of the sexual activity of perfect, monoecious, or dioecious flowers (depending on the plant). With plants, cloning also is possible;

asexual reproduction in plants is generally called vegetative reproduction. Several hybrid types of grass and other plants are sterile and can only be grown from cuttings of parent plants. Asexual reproduction is less prevalent in vegetables, though asparagus and potatoes are generally reproduced this way. More on this later.

Flowering plants (angiosperms) can either be monocots (22 percent of angiosperms) or eudicots (75 percent of angiosperms). The remaining 3 percent is divided between Amborellales, Austrobaileyales, Ceratophyllales, Chloranthales, Magnoliids, and Nymphaeales.[58]

Differentiating one group from another is mainly in the reproductive parts and seed, but can be observed in the leaves, xylem and phloem arrangement, and the plant's main growth point (endosperm). I find the leaf identification method the easiest because monocot leaf veins run lengthwise of the leaf, and dicot leaf veins are striated.

To better understand how sexual propagation works, we're going to explore creating a tomato hybrid from two different plants that show traits that we like in each and want to reproduce in a single plant. Creating strains in your garden is entirely possible. Still, it's worth noting that a single new commercially available hybrid seed is generally the product of years of experimentations and elimination processes. A single winner can have as many as 200,000 competitors during that time.[59]

## Creating a Hybrid

We're using tomato plants in our hybrid experiment, but a pepper plant (also from the Solanaceae family) will work just as well.

Having identified the desired traits in two different tomato cultivars, we will isolate both plants to prevent potential stray pollination. The plants we use need to be super healthy, resilient, and robust. Both plants will act as parent plants, each bearing the fruit of the other. Let's call them Plant A and Plant B. You will use their cultivar names.

Plant A will donate its pollen to an immature (i.e., unpollinated) flower on Plant B, and vice versa. The result will be that both Plant A and Plant B will bear the fruit borne from the pollen of the other. Seed collected from these crossed fruits will be developed separately to identify the one that best reproduces our desired traits and qualities. Below are the steps you need to follow:

### *Preparation*

Identify the plants as per the instructions above and isolate each in different locations and away from all other plants. It is essential that these plants cannot be fertilized by other plants.

You will need the following tools:

- A small pair of scissors, like those used for clipping nails.

- Two sheets of clean printing paper marked with the respective pollen donor's details.

- Four small sealable bags, each marked with variety specifics. Mark two with the details of the parent plant's name and the pollen donator's name, adding the date. Mark the remaining two with the details reversed.

- Tag tape, also showing parent and pollen donator names. You will use these to tag the branch just below the inflorescence being pollinated. When the fruit grows, the tag will help identify its parentage and form part of its children's identification in the following seasons.

- Two fine-point craft paint brushes to transfer the ultra-fine pollen to the stigma. I find cotton ear swabs ineffective as the pollen sticks to them. Use different color brushes and mark each Plant A or Plant B, as applicable.

- Rubbing alcohol to clean the scissors between cuttings on different plants.

Ensure all tools are sterile and the sealable bags have not been used before.

### Cross Fertilization

Using each plant's dedicated fine-tipped paintbrush and a clean sheet of printing paper, collect pollen from Plant A and Plant B, respectively.

Remove all flowers from both tomato plants, leaving only two immature flowers on each plant. Immature flowers still have their bracts (calyx) intact; they are formed but not open. Flower buds, in contrast, don't yet have the bracts visible. Mature flowers, the ones we used to collect pollen from, have their sexual organs exposed, i.e., stamen (male) and pistil (female).

Start by emasculating the chosen immature flower by removing the anther cone. The anther cone is exposed by removing the bracts and the petals and then gently exposing the stigma and the style. Using sterile scissors, carefully remove the anther cone, leaving only the style and stigma. Do this for both immature flowers.

Using the collected pollen from Plant B, fertilize the exposed stigma of the emasculated flowers on Plant A, making the cross. Using a different, clean brush and sterilized scissors, do the same for Plant B.

Because the fertilized stigma is so exposed, cover each emasculated bloom with an appropriately labeled sealable bag to prevent any additional accidental contamination. Take care not to touch or harm the exposed stigma.

Appropriately tag the branches bearing the fertilized pistil to keep track of the fruit from individual crosses.

Once your pollen grains are placed on the stigma, they will move down the style all the way to one of the ovules in the ovary of the flower, fertilizing the ovule and producing a diploid zygote and a triploid endosperm. The endosperm will store food for the embryo.

Once the fruit starts forming, remove the plastic covers, allowing the fruit to mature fully.

Collect the seeds as the plant matures, remembering to keep track of parentage.

F1 hybrids (first generation hybrids) account for most newly released commercial tomatoes, including garden varieties. The seeds you sow in the field the next year are a product of this above-described crossing of two parent plants. Planting the F1 hybrid allows the gardener to take advantage of the greater robustness of the hybrid's highly heterozygous genotype. Seeds saved from any hybrid tomato fruit, whether grown from seed or purchased, are classified as F2 seeds.

### Dehybridizing

By planting your hybrids seeds out and selecting the most vigorous seedlings, growing them to maturity and collecting their seeds for several years, i.e., F2 plants, you will eventually have a stable variety. Dehybridizing develops new pure lines from an existing hybrid through several generations of cultivation, selection, and seed saving.

[above] Here I'm holding a collection of tomato seeds, carefully harvested as a result of a successful hybridization process, illustrating the potential for creating new and unique varieties through the art of plant breeding.

[page left, left] Home hybridization is a fun process. Don't be afraid to experiment.

[page left, right] The intricate beauty of tiny tomato flowers, each one a hermaphroditic wonder, containing both male and female reproductive organs, highlighting the fascinating intricacies of nature and plant reproduction.

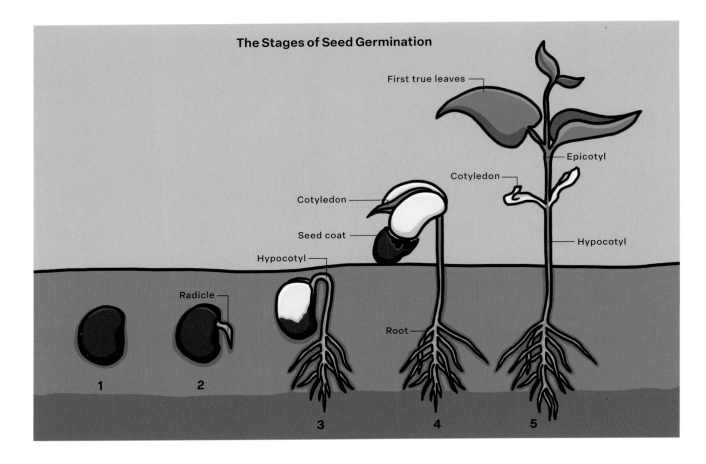

The Stages of Seed Germination

## SEED GERMINATION

A seed cannot sprout unless three requirements are met:

- The embryo must be alive and capable of germination, i.e., the seed must be viable.

- Any physical or chemical internal inhibitors must be removed.

- The seed must be exposed to species-specific environmental factors, such as moisture, adequate temperatures, oxygen, and species-specific light or darkness requirements.

In the illustration above, note the radicle (the initial emerging root), as we'll explore it later when discussing root health. The germination process begins with water absorption, where water quantity and consistency are critical, and a dry spell post-germination can destroy the plant embryo.

Some species' seed germination process is triggered by light (lettuce and dill), so these need to be planted shallowly under lights to optimize germination rates. Most plants germinate best in darkness, and details are generally available on plant packets or leaflets.

Like humans, plants have a circadian clock, requiring some darkness. We review light factors later in this chapter.

Oxygen has not been shown to benefit seed storage, and storage in a vacuum, nitrogen, and carbon dioxide don't affect germination success rates either. During germination, oxygen consumption increases, so ensure adequate supply by using an inert growing media that is light and drains well. Don't use compost or potting soil for seed germination; stick to inert materials such as pumice, perlite, or vermiculite. If you need better anchorage, use coconut coir, which is relatively hygienic when fresh.

A difference between growing media temperatures (higher) and ambient temperatures (lower) helps accelerate seed germination. A ballpark soil temperature is 77°F (25°C), though some members of the cucumber family may need soil temperatures as high as 85°F (29°C) (see page 84). Lower temperatures will merely delay germination and development times.

## Breaking Seed Dormancy

Dormant seeds are viable but inactive, limited by the environment or the seed's physiology (seed-specific inhibitory factors). Physical dormancy can be either internal (endogenous) or external (exogenous). Exogenous dormancy can be eliminated using scarification or stratification techniques.

Vegetable seeds seldom need scarification or exposure to cold temperatures (stratification). Some seeds need a soak to break dormancy—I cover these in the final chapter.

## Limiting Seed Pathogen Transfer

To prevent pathogens from infecting your crops through seeds, you can use hot water to kill them. The water temperature should be around 122°F (50°C) on average, depending on the crop. The average time for soaking the seeds is twenty-five minutes. In the final chapter, I explain how to treat different seeds with hot water. Most seed merchants pretreat available seeds with a fungicide that protects them from diseases. Do not eat these seeds and dispose of the water carefully after use.

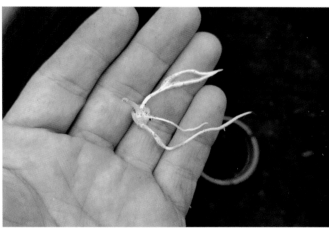

[page left] The vivid color of a red lettuce in the garden. Its rich hues contrast beautifully against the surrounding greenery, offering a visual feast and a delightful addition to the salad bowl.

[top] These four summer squash are placed thoughtfully on a bed of sand, an effective technique employed by gardeners to prevent rotting and ensure a healthy, blemish-free harvest.

[bottom] A pre-sprouted/chitted zucchini seed after undergoing scarification highlights the preparatory process that promotes quicker germination and more successful growth for these popular summer vegetables.

## Asexual Propagation

Artichokes, asparagus, garlic, ginger, gourds, mint, potato, sweet potato, turmeric, onions, and rhubarb can all be propagated vegetatively. Asexual production techniques include cuttings, bulbs, tubers, crown division, and grafting.

It is a quick way of cloning plants. In fact, some hybrids and plants can only be propagated asexually. Garlic, turmeric, and ginger rarely produce viable seeds. Foliar or stem cuttings have genetically identical plants to the parents, while root or seed propagation does not transfer any established mutations such as variegation.

## BOOSTING SOIL HEALTH

While plants are grown without the support of soil, the value of healthy soil to plant well-being and resilience is inimitable. The health of your garden's soil is a product of soil profile, structure, nutrient content, organic matter, biodiversity, and water/air retention capacities. Though I list these separately, they're all interrelated, the one affecting the other. Let's explore each one individually.

## Soil Profile

Roadside excavations give us a glimpse of the Earth's top layers, called soil horizons. The depth of each layer and its arrangement is referred to as the soil's profile, an indicator of the soil's use suitability. A pedosphere with substantial underlying rock formations is excellent for building on but not the best for gardening.

Most gardening soils have four distinct horizons:

- O—Organic surface—up to about 2 feet deep (60 cm) but can extend to 6 feet (183 cm) if soil organisms are encouraged by compost applications.

- A—Surface horizon—up to about 10 feet (3 m) deep. This is generally the cultivated horizon.

- B—Subsoil—up to about 30 feet deep (9 m)

- C—Substratum

- B—Hard bedrock, usually granite, basalt, quartzite, limestone, and sandstone that is cemented together as a rock

There are several other layers, including, L, V, E, R, M, and W, but these are more the domain of pedologists. If you're interested in exploring the subject further, the USDA Soil Survey Manual is a great resource.[60]

[page left, left] The process of dipping seeds into hot water is a simple yet effective technique used to eliminate harmful pathogens and ensure a healthy start for future seedlings and a successful growing season.

[page left, right] The striking beauty of purple potato flowers in full bloom at Simplify Gardening signals the growth phase of the underground tubers and promises a unique and colorful harvest later in the season.

[above] The process of sowing seeds into clay soil illustrates the importance of adapting gardening techniques to suit different soil types and ensure the best possible start for growing plants in various conditions.

The pedosphere includes horizons O and A and can potentially host plants with root systems up to 10 feet (3 m), depending on how it's managed. If your soil doesn't yet offer that, or if you have sandy or clay soil, your best option is to increase organic matter and biodiversity by compost additions. How successfully you transform your soil depends on several factors, but five years of consistent annual compost applications can change your garden's capacity. The deeper a plant's roots can penetrate, the more it is able to access nutrition and develop resilience to fluctuating rain levels.

## Soil Structure

The clay, sand, or silt proportions in your ground vary and determine its soil texture. There are fourteen different soil textures based on these proportions, with loam being a balanced mixture of all three.

The size of the soil particles differs significantly among clay, silt, and sand. If a sand particle is bigger than a baseball, a silt particle is like a pea, and a clay particle is like a pinhead. The texture of the soil affects how it behaves with water, air, compaction, and nutrients.

| Soil Structure Characteristics | | | |
|---|---|---|---|
| **Characteristic** | **Clay** | **Silt** | **Sand** |
| Looseness | Poor | Fair | Good |
| Field Capacity and Saturation Porosity | Poor | Fair | Good |
| Water Management | Poor drainage | Fair | Poor water retention |
| Clod Forming Inclination | Good | Fair | Poor |
| Workability | Poor | Fair | Poor |
| Fertility | Fair to good | Fair | Poor |
| Cation Exchange Capacity (CEC) | Good | Poor | Poor |

A word of caution! Mixing sand and clay doesn't improve your clay's drainage potential. Considering the statement I made above, millions of pinheads can fit around the baseball. Therefore, adding sand has little effect on aeration or water drainage levels. The best way to aerate and enhance clay drainage is by adding compost.

### Fallow Soil—Starting a New Garden

When you've identified a site for vegetable growing, having considered water and light availability, dig a hole of about the width and breadth of a spade and 18 inches (45 cm) deep to check for rocks, and basic soil tilth. If the site is in a community garden or allotment where it was previously cultivated, but has stood unused for a couple of years, and is now covered in die-hard crop residue or weeds, don't worry, we'll sort it out. Farmers will advise you to plow it up and disc it to break clods down, incorporating surface plants back into the soil. It's an option, especially if you have a thousand acres that need to be prepared. For a vegetable garden, there's a better alternative that will deal with any emerging weeds and potential pathogens in the soil but doesn't require disturbing the stabilized pedosphere microbes.

1. Start by selecting your site. To prevent taller plants casting a shadow in smaller plants, run beds in a north to south direction, i.e., perpendicular to the sun's journey from east to west. If the beds are on a slope, consider terracing them.

2. Harvest the flowers and seedpods of the visible weeds— as much as is practical.

3. Cut the remaining plant material down to about 1 inch (2.5 cm) high, or flatten it with a roller or press it down with the back of a rake. You want beds about 10 feet long (3 m) and 4 feet (1.2 m) wide.

See if you can get about six of those, allowing space for paths in between. If the beds are parallel to each other, that's a total size of about 4 by 12 yards (3.6 × 11 m).

Start off by solarizing the whole area you want to use as a garden. If the area is currently covered in turf, scalp it down by mowing it on the mower's lowest setting before you start solarizing it: solarizing is a process of amplifying and trapping the sun's energy under a black plastic sheet that covers the area. A tarp can be used but can be a costly option.

The process should be started whenever you're ready but must stay in place to include at least two months of summer sun. I know, it seems like a waste of precious growing time, but it can save you years of weed-management headaches and the process benefits the soil's biota population. Cover the edges with some ground, and you may need to weigh other parts of the cover down to prevent it from being lifted by gusts of wind. It all depends on your planning and the time available to prepare the garden.

If you don't have a year to prepare the area, the alternative is to invade and partially destroy the soil's ecosystem, allowing you to repopulate it using compost. Rent or buy a rototiller and dig the area up to a depth between 6 to 12 inches (15 to 30 cm).

Start by marking where you want your beds and paths to be and spread 4 to 6 inches (10 to 15 cm) of compost over the areas that will become beds. For six beds of 10 × 4 feet each (3 × 1.2 m; total size 240 sq ft [22.3 m²]), you will need 4.5 cubic yards (3.4 m³) of compost. The amount of

[page left] The persistent growth of weeds in a garden illustrates the importance of regular maintenance and weed control to ensure a healthy and productive growing environment for desired plants.

[top] The significance of orienting garden beds to minimize shadowing, showcasing how thoughtful planning and placement can optimize sunlight exposure and promote the growth and health of the plants in your garden.

[bottom] The use of a sheet placed on the ground to solarize weeds is a clever, eco-friendly method that harnesses the sun's heat to effectively control and eliminate unwanted weeds in the garden.

compost you need depends on how thick you spread it: 1 cubic yard (0.76 m³) covers 54 square feet (5 m²) with a layer of 6 inches (15 cm) but covers 81 square feet (7.5 m²) with a layer of 4 inches (10 cm).

To create raised beds, mix the compost with the soil that has been tilled and removed from the paths. If you have grass, cover it with cardboard sheets on top of the beds and add a mix of compost and soil over them. The cardboard will decompose and kill the grass underneath.

You may have to buy compost or get donations when you start your garden. Ask your municipality for a discount on some compost through its composting program if you agree to use your garden as an example of local home composting. Worm castings and waste compost from commercial mushroom production are good options. Look for the Seal of Testing Assurance (STA) from the US Composting Council when you shop.

## Growing Your First Crop

After creating your raised bed with added compost to boost the soil's biology and carbon content, consider further strengthening your soil's crop growth potential by planting one of the plants from the Fabaceae family or the list below. Legumes fix nitrogen from the air and also are effective at managing lesion nematodes[61]:

- Alfalfa

- Alsike clover

- Buckwheat (non-legume)

- Crown vetch

- Hairy vetch

- Oats (non-legume)

- Canola (Brassica)

- Red clover

- Ryegrass (non-legume)

- Sudan grass (non-legume)

- Phacelia (non-legume, pollinator favorite and great for improving water infiltration, and potassium content)

- Wheat (non-legume)

- White clover

Follow this with a snap bean crop to further boost the soil's natural nitrogen content and health. Plant the beans in the cover crop's residue without tilling it in. Just cut it down or flatten it so that it acts as a mulch. Start your garden with a mindset that abhors exposed ground, keeping all soil perpetually covered. Only clear a foot-square space for the bean seedling.

Also consider planting plants from the Verbenaceae family along the verges of your garden as these attract beneficial insects that will help you in your pest control efforts. The most common garden verbenas in North American gardens are a lilac vervain *Verbena rigida* and hybrid verbena *V. × hybrida*. Flowers improve natural or biological management by luring and supporting the presence of many pests' natural enemies in the garden. Ladybugs, green lacewings, tachinid flies, syrphid flies, and parasitic wasps are only some of the plethora of useful insects that frequent flowers.

Here's a list of thirty plants known to attract ladybugs, green lacewings, tachinid flies, syrphid flies, and parasitic wasps, all natural enemies to common garden pests:

- Alfalfa
- Basket-of-gold
- Big flower vetch
- Blanket flower
- Buckwheat
- Caraway
- Cinquefoil
- Coneflower
- Coreopsis
- Cilantro (Coriander)
- Cosmos
- Dill
- Fava bean
- Fennel
- Goldenrod
- Hairy vetch
- Hoary alyssum
- Milkweeds
- Mustards
- Phacelia
- Queen Anne's lace
- Sunflower
- Sweet alyssum
- Sweet clover
- Tansy
- Toothpick weed
- Wild mustard
- Wild parsnip
- Yarrow
- Yellow rocket

[page left, left] Unintentional damage is caused to the soil ecosystem when digging in the garden. The need for mindful gardening practices to preserve the delicate balance of microorganisms and nutrients vital for plant growth is essential.

[page left, right] Here, I'm adding wheelbarrows full of nutrient-rich compost to a garden bed within the homemade tunnel, showcasing the importance of feeding the soil and supporting the microbial life that contributes to healthy, thriving plants.

[right] The lush growth of a green manure cover crop consisting of field beans and hairy vetch, effectively enriches and protects the soil while promoting sustainable gardening practices.

### *Test the Soil*

For accurate sample taking instructions, as well as test kits and report forms, contact your county's Agricultural Extension service office. They can advise you on how much lime and fertilizer your garden needs to optimize nutrition and pH levels. Adjust fallow ground fertility months in advance before using the space for growing vegetables.

## OPTIMIZING PLANT BIOLOGY

Optimizing plant biology requires us to consider the structure, function, growth, evolution, and ecology of plants. Plants are multicellular organisms that use photosynthesis to produce their own food (photoautotrophs). Plants have different types of organs that perform different roles.

- Roots anchor the plant in the soil and absorb water and minerals.

- Meristems are regions of plant tissue where cell division and growth occur.

- Stems support the plant and transport water and nutrients. Covered stems also can produce rhizomes (often called stolons) from which tubers grow.

- Leaves are the main site of photosynthesis and gas exchange.

- Nodes are the points where leaves or branches attach to the stem.

- Buds are undeveloped shoots that can grow into new stems or flowers.

## Roots

The root system of vegetable plants is part of the plant that grows underground and performs various functions, such as anchoring the plant, absorbing water and minerals, conducting nutrients to the stem, and storing food. Multiple types of roots and root systems exist among vegetable plants, depending on their structure, depth, and origin.

The radicle is the first root to emerge from the germinating seed, growing in the direction of gravity to become a taproot or fibrous root. A taproot is a thick main root that has smaller lateral roots branching from it. Fibrous roots are a mass of thin roots that emerges from the base of the stem (potatoes and grasses are good examples).

Another category of roots is adventitious roots. These arise from a different place on a plant, usually a stem or a leaf. They are the reason you can vegetatively propagate plants from cuttings or grafts. Some plants can form aerial roots that hang in the air or grow upward out of the soil for submerged roots. Examples of vegetable plants with adventitious roots are tomatoes and potatoes, which grow adventitious roots along their stems when buried. Potatoes also grow rhizomes from the stem on which they grow tubers.

A third root classification refers to root depth. Roots can be shallow-rooted (less than 12 inches [30 cm]), medium-rooted (7 to 24 inches [18 to 60 cm]), or deep-rooted (more than 30 inches [76 cm]). Knowing the root depth of vegetable plants can help plot a garden by choosing appropriate watering schedules, containers, or raised beds. It also can help avoid plant competition by pairing a plant with others that have different root depths.

[left] These four bean plants in root trainers reveal their strong and healthy root systems, which are essential for the plants' ability to absorb nutrients and water, resulting in robust growth and a successful harvest.

[page right, top] Here I am skillfully potting on a potato seedling with a robust root system, ensuring the young plant's healthy growth and preventing it from becoming root-bound as it outgrows its original container.

[page right, bottom] In this photo, I'm holding up a gutter full of healthy pea seedlings, expertly grown and now ready to be transplanted into the garden for a successful crop of delicious, homegrown peas.

For example, shallow-rooted plants, such as lettuce, may do better in clay-based soil that retains moisture near the surface; medium-rooted plants, such as cabbage, may need loamy soil that drains well; deep-rooted plants, such as pumpkins, may require soil with high organic matter that allows air circulation deeper down. Some examples of shallow-rooted vegetables are spinach, radish, and green onion; some examples of medium-rooted vegetables are broccoli, cauliflower, and carrot; some examples of deep-rooted vegetables are asparagus, squash, and pumpkin.

### Optimizing Root Health

Optimizing vegetable plant root health is essential for achieving high yields and quality. Root health depends on several factors, such as soil structure, moisture, nutrients, pH, temperature, and biological activity. To improve root health follow these best practices:

- Choose well-adapted varieties that are resistant or tolerant to root diseases and pests.

- Prepare the soil properly by adding organic matter, improving drainage, and avoiding compaction.

- Apply balanced fertilizers according to soil-test results and crop needs; avoid overfertilization that can cause salt accumulation and root burn.

- Water the plants regularly and deeply, but not excessively, to maintain optimal soil moisture levels and prevent drought stress or waterlogging.

- Control weeds that can compete with the plants for water and nutrients and harbor root pathogens and insects.

- Rotate crops with different root systems and nutrient requirements and avoid planting the same or related crops in the same spot for several years.

- Monitor the plants for signs of root problems, such as wilting, yellowing, stunting, or poor growth, and take appropriate measures to diagnose and treat them.

Following these practices, vegetable growers can protect their plants' roots and ensure optimal yield and quality.

## Meristems

Meristems are regions of plant tissues that consist of actively dividing cells. They are responsible for the growth and development of various plant organs, such as roots, stems, leaves, and flowers. Different types of meristems are based on their location and function in the plant.

Apical meristems are found at the tips of roots and shoots and produce primary tissues that increase the length of the plant. Lateral meristems are located along the sides of stems and roots and produce secondary tissues that increase the thickness of the plant. Intercalary meristems are found at the bases of leaves or internodes, allowing for rapid growth and regrowth of some plants, such as grasses. Meristematic cells are usually small and densely packed, with thin cell walls, large nuclei, and small or no vacuoles.

Vegetable plants have meristems that enable them to grow and produce new organs throughout their life cycle. Some vegetables can be regenerated from their meristems even after being harvested or cut. For example, the shoots of root vegetables such as carrots and beets can sprout new leaves from their apical meristems if placed in water or moist soil. However, the roots of carrots and beets cannot regrow as the root meristem, located at the beet or carrot root tip, has been removed.

Leafy vegetables such as lettuce and celery can regrow new leaves from their intercalary meristems if their bases are left intact and exposed to water and light. Some vegetables can propagate vegetatively from their lateral meristems, such as potatoes that can grow new tubers from their eyes or stem segments.

## Stems

Stems are essential to vegetable plants, as they support the leaves, flowers and fruits, and they transport water and nutrients throughout the plant. Stems also store food and water for the plant, and some stems can produce new plants through vegetative propagation. Stem health depends on several factors, such as the type of stem (herbaceous or woody), environmental conditions (light, temperature, humidity, airflow, and $CO_2$ levels), pests and diseases, and pruning and harvesting practices.

The phloem and xylem are part of the vascular tissues in plant stems. They have different functions and structures, but they work together to transport water, minerals, and organic substances throughout the plant. Phloem transports sugars and other products of photosynthesis from the leaves to the roots and other parts of the plant.

Xylem is composed of tracheids and vessel elements, and it transports water and dissolved minerals from the roots to the leaves and other parts of the plant. The phloem and xylem are arranged in bundles in the stem, usually alternating with each other. The position of these bundles varies depending on the type of stem. In herbaceous stems, the bundles are scattered throughout the stem. In woody stems, the bundles form concentric rings called annual rings. The growth of new xylem cells adds to the thickness of the stem, forming wood.

[page left, left] The apical meristem is found at the very tip of the shoot (or root) system, and it's where new cells are formed that will increase the height/length of the plant.

[page left, right] Stems are essential for supporting the leaves and fruits, and they also contain the vessel elements that move water and nutrients throughout a plant.

[page right, top] Nodes are the points on a stem where leaves, flowers, or fruits emerge. Pruning your plants can encourage (or discourage, as the case may be) node growth to create different branching structures and growth habitats.

[page right, bottom] I'm sitting proudly beside a bed of garlic, ready for harvest. The entire bed is dedicated to a single, flourishing crop of garlic, illustrating the success of focused and attentive gardening.

## Nodes and Buds

Managing nodes and buds to optimize vegetable plant health is essential for gardeners and farmers. Nodes are the points on a stem where leaves, branches, or flowers emerge. Buds are undeveloped shoots that can grow into new stems or flowers. You can control certain vegetable plants' shape, size, and productivity by pruning or pinching off some of the nodes and buds. Pruning can help prevent diseases and pests by improving air circulation and removing damaged parts.

Some of the benefits of managing nodes and buds are:

- Increasing fruit size and quality by directing more energy and nutrients to the remaining fruits

- Encouraging branching and bushiness by stimulating the growth of lateral buds

- Enhancing flavor and aroma by reducing the number of flowers and leaves that compete with the fruits for resources

- Extending the harvest season by delaying flowering and fruiting

Different vegetable plants have different pruning needs and methods. For example, tomatoes are usually pruned to remove suckers, the shoots that grow between the main stem and a branch. Peppers often are pinched at the top to encourage branching and more peppers. Cucumbers are pruned to remove excess vines and leaves that can shade the fruits. Beans and peas are usually not pruned; they produce more pods when left alone.

You should always use sharp and clean tools to prune your vegetable plants and avoid pruning when the plants are wet or stressed.

[left] This photo captures the moment I planted a giant cabbage grown from seed, which would later develop into an impressive 67-pound (30 kg) cabbage, with lots of large, healthy leaves.

[page right] By carefully picking the outer leaves of various lettuce varieties from a garden bed, you're practicing a sustainable harvesting method and you can enjoy fresh salads throughout the season.

## Leaves

Leaves are the main organ of photosynthesis in plants and have several functions essential for plant survival and growth. Some of the main functions of leaves are:

**Photosynthesis:** Leaves use chlorophyll, a green pigment, to absorb light energy and convert carbon dioxide and water into glucose, a type of sugar. Glucose is then transported to other parts of the plant through the phloem, a tube system that carries sap. Photosynthesis also produces oxygen, which is released into the air through pores called stomata. Photosynthesis is the primary source of food and energy for plants and most living organisms on Earth.

**Transpiration:** Leaves also lose water through stomata when they open for gas exchange. This process of water loss is called transpiration, and it helps to cool the plant and maintain its water balance. Transpiration also creates a suction force that draws water and minerals from the roots to the leaves through the xylem, another tube system that carries sap.

**Guttation:** When the soil is very moist, and the stomata are closed at night, leaves may exude drops of water from special glands at their edges or tips. This process is called guttation, and it helps to relieve the pressure that builds up in the xylem due to water absorption by the roots.

**Storage:** Some leaves can store food, water, or other substances in their tissues. For example, cacti have thick and fleshy leaves that store water to survive in dry environments. Onions have modified leaves that store carbohydrates in their bulbs. Some plants have leaves that produce latex, resin, or oil for defense or attraction.

**Exchange of gases:** Leaves allow plants to exchange gases with the atmosphere. Besides oxygen and carbon dioxide, leaves may release or take in other gases such as water vapor, ethylene, methane, or ozone. These gases can affect the growth, development, or response of plants to their environment.

## Foliar Health

The total soluble solids in the plant sap, a gauge of photosynthetic activity and plant health, is measured as Brix by using a tool known as a refractometer. Measuring Brix levels is helpful because it very quickly gives us an idea of the plant's health and resilience to pests, diseases, and extreme climatic conditions. A refractometer measures the refraction of dissolved content in liquids, mainly sugars. However, many other chemicals may be present and contribute some small factor to the Brix reading, such as lipids, amino acids, and suspended particles or colloids.

## *Leaves as Indicators of Plant Health*

Plants can communicate their distress through various changes in their leaves. Some common leaf signs that indicate a plant is in distress are:

**Wilting:** This can be caused by lack of water, excess water, root damage, extreme heat or cold, or disease. Check the soil moisture and temperature, and adjust accordingly. If the problem persists, inspect the roots for signs of rot or injury.

**Bleaching:** This can be caused by sunburn, especially for plants not used to direct sunlight. Move the plant to a shadier spot or cover it with a sheer curtain. The plant may outgrow minor sunburn, but severe damage may require pruning.

**Blackening:** This can be caused by frost damage, which kills and turns the plant cells black. Cover the plant with a frost cloth or bring it indoors if possible. Remove the damaged leaves after the frost has passed and the plant shows new growth.

**Raggedness:** This can be caused by wind, rain, hail, insects, or animals. The torn leaves make the plant more vulnerable to disease, so removing them and protecting them from further damage is best. Use a garden fabric or a net to shield the plant from harsh weather or pests.

**Off-color:** This can be caused by nutrient deficiency, which affects chlorophyll production and leaf color. Pale leaves may indicate a lack of nitrogen, while yellow leaves with green veins may indicate a lack of iron. Reddish or purplish leaves may indicate a lack of phosphorus. Apply a balanced fertilizer according to the plant's needs and soil-test results.

## Improving Photosynthesis

While photosynthesis often is thought of as dependent on water, light, and $CO_2$, the whole process can be improved if we start with soil health. Effective photosynthesis also improves soil health, stimulating a cyclic process of perpetual growth and environmental improvement. But, as with the chicken and the egg paradox, it starts with healthy biodiversity-rich soil and has enough nutrients, specifically nitrogen, phosphorus, manganese, iron, boron, and magnesium. Given this start in life, plants will grow stronger and more resilient to soilborne pathogens. As the photosynthesis system improves, more complex polysaccharide sugars such as cellulose, pectin, lignin, and starches are produced.

Improved photosynthesis perpetuates the strengthening of other systems as more significant amounts of plant sugars are transferred through the roots to feed soil microbes. That, in turn, makes more minerals available to the plant. Acting as coenzymes, increased mineral availability helps strengthen the plant's nitrogen-conversion-to-proteins process. A higher protein level is an effective antidote to plant insects that prefer simple foods. Finding a balance between plant systems, soil biology, and the full spectrum of nutrient availability is key to growing plants resistant to pests, diseases, and climatic extremes.

As we will see in the next section, weakness attracts attacks, and conversely, strength develops resilience and perpetuates improved strength. As your plants flourish, their sugar and protein contents improve and diversify, strengthening soil microbes that release a higher quality of nutrients as they reduce complex elements to bioavailable forms. The strength and diversity of your soil's microbial populations are crucial to your plants' optimal health, a state that is even resistant to airborne bacterial and fungal attacks. Extreme plant health is even immune to beetle attacks.

## Talking Leaves

Plants use different methods to send and receive signals, such as chemicals, electrical pulses, and fungi networks. These signals help plants to share information, cooperate, compete, and defend themselves from threats.

One way that plants communicate is through chemicals that they secrete into the soil or the air. These chemicals can affect the growth and behavior of other plants nearby. For example, some plants release toxins that inhibit the growth of their neighbors, while others release hormones that stimulate their allies. Some plants can warn each other of insect attacks by emitting volatile compounds that repel herbivores or attract predators.

Another way that plants communicate is through electrical pulses that travel along their roots and stem. These pulses can carry information about the plant's condition, such as stress, damage, or nutrient availability. Scientists have found that plants can sense when their leaves are touched by another plant and respond by changing their growth strategy. Some plants can detect the presence of their kin and adjust their resource allocation accordingly.

A third way that plants communicate is through fungi networks that connect their roots underground. These networks, called mycorrhizae, allow plants to exchange nutrients and information. Plants can send signals through these networks to help each other cope with drought, disease, or shade. They can share warnings about pests and predators.

Plants are not silent or passive organisms. They have complex ways of communicating with each other that we are only beginning to understand. By studying how plants talk to each other, we can learn more about their ecology, evolution, and intelligence.

## DISEASE MANAGEMENT

Plant pathogens, i.e., fungi, bacteria, viruses, and nematodes, cause plant diseases. Plant disease requires three components: pathogen(s), a vulnerable host, and a disease-friendly environment. Good hygiene and cultural management are effective defense strategies; as far as plant diseases go, you don't want an infection to get a foothold. Insects are a fourth component of the illness cycle. These components are your disease-prevention goals; eliminating one to reduce plant disease risks.

I cover plant-family-specific diseases in the last chapter.

### How to Diagnose Plant Diseases

It is essential to properly diagnose plant diseases before implementing any management strategies. Some diseases may appear similar but require different treatment methods so that a correct diagnosis can save time and money. Additionally, pathogens vary in their survival and spread strategies so some management techniques may be effective for some diseases but not others.

It's also important to note that disease control products are usually specific to certain disorders, as fungicides do not work against viruses. Some fungi can help treat certain diseases but not others. Furthermore, not all microorganisms that cause plant diseases are fungi, as oomycetes such as Pythium, Phytophthora, and downy mildews exist.

Lastly, it's worth noting that materials used to manage one disease may not work on another and that different approaches are required for root, leaf spots, and fruit diseases. Finally, several non-disease factors, such as environmental stress, nutritional problems, herbicide injuries, and air pollution, can imitate plant diseases.

Here are some general steps to follow when you think a pathogen is to blame for poor plant performance:

**Observe the plant:** Look for signs of disease on the leaves, stems, fruit, and roots of the plant. Take note of any discoloration, spots, deformities, or abnormalities.

**Research the problem:** Use online resources, gardening books, and local gardening experts to identify common diseases that affect the particular vegetable plant. This will help you narrow down the possibilities.

**Take a sample:** If you can't identify the disease based on visual inspection, take a sample of the affected plant tissue (leaves, stem, or fruit) and bring it to a local gardening center or Extension office for analysis.

[top] Resilient, healthy plants are the result of resilient, healthy soils and effective photosynthesis.

[bottom] Plant diseases can affect just about any vegetable plant, but prevention and management techniques can help. This pea plant is suffering from powdery mildew.

**Test the soil:** Test the soil to determine if any nutrient deficiencies or imbalances could contribute to the disease.

**Treat the disease:** Once you have identified the disease, research the appropriate treatment. Depending on the disease, treatment may include removing infected plants, applying fungicides or pesticides, or adjusting the soil pH or nutrient levels.

Always use proper safety precautions when handling plant material and chemicals, and consult with a professional if you are unsure about the best course of action.

## Water and Humidity Management

Reading the above may leave you feeling hopeless in managing diseases. Of central importance in disease management is the quality of your soil. Wet environments should be avoided as they are ideal for many bacterial and fungal diseases. Wet soils with inadequate drainage are favorable to some soilborne pathogen species, including Phytophthora and Pythium. Planting shouldn't be done in areas with recognized drainage issues. Consider using raised beds and improving drainage.

High humidity and moist plant surfaces are optimal for several leaf spot and fruit rot diseases. Leaf wetness can be decreased by using drip irrigation rather than overhead irrigation. If you utilize overhead irrigation, water early, so the plant surfaces are completely dry before dusk. Avoid overhead irrigation in the evening.

Reduce the number of plants in an area to improve airflow and sunshine penetration, reducing leaf wetness and humidity. Appropriate staking or trellising will promote airflow with some crops (such as tomatoes). Airflow can be improved by reducing the number of weeds in and around the crop. Arrange the rows to get the most airflow and sunlight.

Use fans or passive ventilation in greenhouses and high tunnels to lower humidity. Don't work on soggy soil.

## Crop Rotation Limitations

Crop rotation and fall tillage are practical disease management strategies if a pathogen survives in crop residue or soil. Once plant debris decomposes, pathogens die, and fall tillage controls illnesses by lowering pathogen winter survival. Rotating crops helps control diseases by preventing plant pathogen buildup in the soil. Don't plant sequential crops from the same botanical family in the same bed.

Unfortunately, crop rotation doesn't affect some soilborne diseases. First, infections build durable survival structures that endure time and nonhost crops (Fusarium wilt and root-knot nematode). Another set of illnesses unaffected by crop rotation can survive permanently on numerous crop and weed species (Sclerotia, Rhizoctonia, and Verticillium). The root-knot nematode can infect cucurbits, tomatoes, carrots, and weeds.

Before making judgments, consider all options. Rotation promotes soil tilth, but fall tillage often goes against suggested soil management and conservation methods. If you implement no-till or restricted tillage practices, you must be more diligent with other disease-prevention techniques.

This cucumber plant in the greenhouse is affected by powdery mildew, a common fungal disease. The visible white, powdery spots serve as a reminder to monitor plant health and implement preventive measures to protect the garden's productivity.

## Healthy Plant Material

Saving vegetable seeds for next year's crop is not suggested unless you are skilled in seed sanitation; we'll explore this in more detail later. When a seed-borne disease is active, don't keep seeds. Check seedlings often and remove a few plants from containers to investigate their roots. Keep transplants apart from other plants and the producing area for a few days to prevent disease spread. Ask your plant suppliers about disease prevention, and if you detect disease on received plants, take photos, and call the supplier or pathogen diagnostic lab. (This is available via many university Agricultural Extension centers.)

## Disease-Resistant Varieties

Plant disease-resistant cultivars whenever possible. There may not be totally disease-proof options available, but there may be ones with varying degrees of protection. Tolerance may be mentioned in seed catalogs. There are rootstocks for some vegetables (e.g., tomatoes) that have evolved resistance to specific soilborne diseases. If you want to plant a tomato variety that is sensitive to soilborne diseases, but you have a history of that disease in your soil, planting a grafted tomato plant that combines a scion (shoot system) of that desired variety with a resistant rootstock may be a good option.

## PEST MANAGEMENT

Vegetable pest management is the practice of preventing and controlling the damage caused by insects, diseases, weeds, and other pests that affect vegetable crops. It involves using a combination of cultural, biological, physical, and chemical methods to reduce pest populations and protect crop quality and yield. Vegetable pest management also aims to minimize the environmental and health risks associated with pesticide use.

Rotating crops can help prevent pathogen buildup.

## Insect Pests

Vegetable plants can be attacked by different types of insect pests that cause damage and reduce yield. Some of the most common types are:

**Chewing insects:** These insects have strong mouthparts that allow them to bite and chew through plant tissues. They can feed on leaves, stems, roots, fruits, or seeds. Some examples of chewing insects are caterpillars, beetles, grasshoppers, and snails.

**Sucking insects:** These insects have piercing-sucking mouthparts that enable them to suck out the sap or juice from plant cells. They can cause wilting, yellowing, stunting, or distortion of plant parts. Some examples of sucking insects are aphids, whiteflies, thrips, and scale insects.

**Disease-spreading insects:** These insects may not directly damage the plant but can transmit viruses, bacteria, or fungi that cause diseases. They can create wounds or openings that allow pathogens to enter the plant. Some examples of disease-spreading insects are aphids, leafhoppers, psyllids, mealybugs, and mites.

## Cultural Practices

Keeping plants healthy and limiting stress helps them repair insect or mite damage. As we saw earlier, a healthy plant that gets optimal nutrition, lives in healthy soil filled with diverse biota, and can maximize photosynthesis is quite resilient to pest attacks.

Cultural pest management techniques are methods that aim to make the crop environment less suitable for insect pests by manipulating the growing system or cultural practices. Some of the common cultural pest management techniques for vegetable plant insect pests are:

**Sanitation:** This involves destroying or removing crop residue, spilled seeds, weeds, volunteer plants, and other sources of pest habitat in and around the crop. Sanitation can reduce or eliminate pest populations that overwinter or breed in these habitats. Sanitation also is important in storage and processing facilities to prevent pest infestation and spread.

[top] This close-up photo reveals two whitefly pests on a leaf, showcasing their tiny, sap-sucking mouthparts. This image highlights the importance of monitoring for pests and implementing effective control methods to ensure a healthy garden.

[bottom] Here you can see numerous aphids feeding on a plant stem. When numerous, aphids can leave behind a sticky residue, upon which molds can grow. Watch out for aphids as the damage they can inflict on plants is extensive, particularly if in large numbers.

**Crop rotation:** This involves planting different crops in a sequence to disrupt the life cycle of pests that are specific to particular host plants. Crop rotation can reduce pest populations and damage by depriving them of their preferred food source and exposing them to natural enemies.

**Planting date adjustment:** This involves timing the planting of crops to avoid peak periods of pest activity or to take advantage of favorable environmental conditions. Planting date adjustment can reduce pest pressure and damage by minimizing crop exposure to pests or enhancing resistance to pests.

**Reflective mulches:** These are mulches that reflect ultraviolet light and repel incoming insects from alighting on plants. Reflective mulches are usually aluminum-based and are effective against insect pests that transmit viruses, such as aphids, thrips, and whiteflies. Reflective mulches can reduce the incidence of virus-infected plants by interfering with the vector-host interaction.

**Physical barriers:** These are materials that prevent or limit the access of pests to crops. Physical barriers include row covers, netting, fencing, sticky bands, and trapping devices. Physical barriers can protect crops from insect pests, wildlife, and birds that may cause damage or spread diseases.

Cultural methods often are used as a preventive measure and can be combined with other integrated pest management strategies for optimal results.

Now that we've discussed some useful methods for optimizing plant health through proper propagation, boosting soil health, managing pests and diseases, and improving plant biological healthy by understanding the parts of a plant and how they function, it's time to turn our attention to providing proper nutrition to our vegetable plants.

Planting potatoes even a few weeks later than usual can be enough to deter Colorado potato beetles. Planting to avoid the life cycle of pests is one cultural practice that can make your garden more resilient.

A diverse vegetable garden is essential to the regenerative approach.

# Chapter 5:
## Optimizing Plant Nutrition

The previous two chapters reviewed the eleven factors that affect plant growth, the elements contributing to plant health, and risk mitigation. This chapter explores plant nutrition optimization with a focus on creating sustainable food systems.

### REGENERATIVE GARDENING PRINCIPLES

An earlier chapter of this book explored the interconnectedness of separate systems and their combined contribution to the Earth's capacity to sustain life. There's a growing awareness that our behavioral impact is hastening us toward tipping points beyond which recovery is unlikely.[62]

According to the United States EPA, agricultural activities are part of the problem and contribute 11 percent of greenhouse gas emissions.[63] The flip side is that novel farming practices such as regenerative agriculture can cut emissions and become a carbon dioxide sponge, reversing damages.

Various regenerative farming models have emerged, and one can expect further adaptations as contexts,

productivity needs, and practicalities change. The essential regenerative gardening principles include:

- Encourage diversity of plants, biota, and animals.
- Protect the ecosystem from damage.
- Preserve nature's organic purity.
- Boost soil carbon content.

### Principle 1:
### Facilitate Organic Diversity

Diversity in and on the soil is a break from the belief that monocropping is the most effective way to economically meet our food needs. Diversity encourages inter-species symbiotic effects, promotes healthy competition, and enhances resilience.[64]

#### Plant Diversity

Rather than planting a single crop and fighting to manage weed emergence, the regenerative approach includes complementary plants that support the main crop. An example is intercropping with the Fabaceae family to boost nitrogen

[above] Adding slow-release fertilizer to my containers before planting potatoes ensures equal distribution. The containers are neatly arranged in the background, ready to be filled with soil and planted.

[page right] This image captures a rototiller in action, churning up the soil in a vegetable garden. The image showcases the process of preparing the ground for new plantings and incorporating organic matter into the soil. Tilling, however, should not be a regular practice in established garden beds.

fixation, eliminate the need for weeding, act as a green mulch, and leave a nitrous plant residue in the soil at the season's end. Several trees and shrubs also help extract nitrogen from the atmosphere and channel it into the ground, making it available for plant growth—I explain how in the plant nutrient section of this chapter.

## Soil Biota

Biologically diverse communities increase the likelihood of having a species more adept at managing challenges within the system, thus increasing the community's survival chances. Diversity is a proven factor in increased systemic resilience, and crop diversity offers the same benefits.

For those interested in this exciting field of study, check out the Soil Biodiversity Observation Network (SoilBON).[65]

A healthy soil biota would consist of the following:

- An abundant, diverse soil biota population
- Soil biota communities around roots in diverse habitats
- Functional and taxonomical diversity
- Soil biomass
- Decomposing organic matter
- Soil respiration
- Enzymatic activity
- Soil aggregation
- Nutrient cycling

## Introducing Biodiversity

Adding quality compost to the soil is the easiest way to boost biological diversity below ground. An alternative method is actively aerated compost tea (AACT) applications, where fungi-bacteria ratios can be manipulated by adding proteins (fungi booster) or carbohydrates (bacteria booster) during the aeration process. A third method uses specially formulated biodiversity boosters, such as the Effective Microorganisms (EM-1®) used in Bokashi composting.

## Principle 2:
## Protect the Pedosphere from Harm

The most valuable asset a gardener has is their soil, and protecting it can be divided into four interrelated strategies:

- Erosion prevention
- Minimizing water loss
- Soil biota preservation
- Preventing soil compaction

Often these are all lumped under the banner of no-till, but the topic is broader and a bit more complicated.

### Soil Erosion

Erosion is a product of force on the soil surface, either by water or wind. A winning strategy to prevent soil erosion is strengthening aggregate formation, a product of bioactivity. Sufficient ground cover and roots incorporated into aggregates support soil stability and reduce surface water flow rates. Offsetting the angle of sloped beds helps slow water flow speeds, allowing for better infiltration and reducing the risk of erosion.

### Protecting the Biome

No-till aims to limit the destruction of soil biology, allowing it to stabilize and flourish, as best evidenced by the presence of earthworms. However, if your garden is compacted, allowing only limited water infiltration, then tillage intervention is justified. Water infiltration levels of less than 1 inch (2.5 cm) per hour is a sure sign that the soil's carbon content and microorganism activity are below par. Microorganisms are the primary constructors of soil aggregates that enhance soil porosity. If you are totally opposed to tilling soil, you can remedy compacted soil by annual applications of 4 to 6 inches (10 to 15 cm) of compost on the surface. Building contractors and mining companies commonly use this approach to revitalize sites. An interesting longitudinal study of topical compost applications is the Marin Carbon Project in California.[66]

## Principle 3: Preserve Organic Purity

Regenerative gardening allows nature to regenerate its own health, best achieved in forests where humans seldom present a problem. My grandfather, my mentor, often used to say: "A little knowledge is a dangerous thing." In our efforts to "help," we often interfere with natural processes, interrupting food cycles and creating havoc in finely balanced systems.

We would do better if we did less. Purity implies limiting foreign synthetic additions such as pesticides, herbicides, fungicides, and excessive synthetic fertilizers.

By adding waste vegetables to a Bokashi bin, then covering them with bran, I'm using an effective and eco-friendly method of recycling kitchen waste and turning it into nutrient-rich compost for gardening purposes.

## Principle 4: Up the Carbon Content

As mentioned, the Earth's atmosphere comprises only 0.04 percent carbon dioxide, with nitrogen at 78 percent and oxygen at 11 percent. The challenge with atmospheric carbon dioxide ($CO_2$) is its propensity to trap heat, creating the greenhouse effect. While transport, industries, and electricity generation contribute vast quantities, according to the EPA, agriculture contributes 11 percent. This is mainly due to poor farming practices. Regenerative farming practices allow farms to become carbon sinks, absorbing and storing copious amounts of $CO_2$.[67]

Plants do this through photosynthesis, which makes $CO_2$ available as soil organic carbon (SOC). Microorganisms feed on this carbon, strengthening population diversity, improving soil health, and improving crop sustainability.

Additions of carbon-based organic materials, such as compost or biochar, strengthen microorganism populations and further increase the soil's ability to absorb $CO_2$.

Healthy soil should have at least 4 percent soil organic carbon (SOC) content.

### COMPOSTING

Composting is probably the least appreciated and most beneficial of all the gardening strategies. If it is done onsite, the benefits are even more substantial as the organisms responsible for the process are more resilient to local pathogens, a trait passed on to local crops. Composting is the term used to define organic matter's purposeful and managed decomposition process (materials containing carbon molecules).[68] There are several decomposition processes, mainly characterized by the presence or absence of oxygen. Organic material can be decomposed in fermentation (consider the approach used in Bokashi composting).

## Composting Benefits

A whole book can be written on the benefits of composting. Below is a list of reasons why composting is an essential skill set every gardener should develop.[69][70][71][72]

- Managed composting is the most effective way to benefit from the natural decomposition process, introducing prolific populations of microorganisms into gardens.

- Composting allows thermophilic bacteria and fungi to thrive at high temperatures, +160°F (71°C), above the thermal survival threshold of seeds and common troublesome pathogens.

- Composting boosts the population and diversity of a tiered hierarchy of soil predators and prey. Nitrogen is absorbed and stored in the lower-order consumption of materials and organisms. At the same time, carbon is consumed and burnt off, releasing $CO_2$. The result is the sequential conversion of nutrients to a form that plants can use. We're all allergic to the above statement "releasing $CO_2$," but the atmosphere only contains 0.04 percent $CO_2$, an essential component of photosynthesis. $CO_2$ released in the proximity of plants is used by those plants to produce their food.

- In clay, compost reduces anaerobic conditions by decreasing density and increasing porosity. Sand benefits from compost as it improves texture and strengthens aggregate formation. Silt is aerated, reducing its tendency toward being a dilatant fluid.

- Organisms in compost produce a glue-like compound that binds soil grains, preventing erosion. Improved hydrophilic action is a function of fungi and reduces the loss of nutrients through leaching. Air, moisture, and nutrients are all held together in the soil's many tiny air channels and pores.

- Compost adds organic matter, which is essential for improved cation exchange capacity (CEC). CEC is a soil capacity to attract, retain, and incrementally release plant moisture and nutrition. The low CEC of sand allows water to flow through it twenty times faster than other soils.

- Soil microbes have demonstrated their ability to replenish leached or lost nutrients over time. In most cases, this process occurs over two to three years. Improved conditions for soil microbes, such as more food (carbon), air, and water, and less habitat disruption, can help the soil function better.

- Compost with balanced microorganism populations can be enhanced by combining applications with green composting, the growth of legumes such as vetch or trefoil plants. Rhizobia, mycorrhizae, actinomycetes, diazotrophic bacteria and other rhizosphere microorganisms have symbiotic relations with these plants and help fixate atmospheric nitrogen into the soil.

- Aerobic composting has a pH buffering function able to adapt soil acidity to environmental requirements. The microorganisms cause the pH to fluctuate between 5.5 and 7.2.

- During composting, chemicals are reduced from complex compounds into bioavailable monomers (e.g., monosaccharides, amino acids, etc.). The activity also involves re-synthesis and polymerization reactions to produce a product that is intricately beneficial to soil health and plant life.

- The composting process reduces and redefines organic matter. Even though a compost pile may start with a carbon-to-nitrogen ratio of 30:1, the product could be as low as 10:1. This implies a greater concentration of nutritious nitrogen per volume.

## Types of Composting

I'm not going into the detail about the different composting processes, but here are options to consider.

**Traditional composting:** an aerobic process of cyclic heating and turning while keeping the batch damp and aerated. We'll explore this in some detail below.

**Anaerobic composting:** anaerobic composting is done without oxygen and produces methane gas. The sludge residue is generally higher in nitrogen content than traditional composting, but that's about the only advantage.

**Bokashi composting:** the process of fermenting kitchen scraps (usually in an enclosed container) to produce an exceptional compost loaded with effective microorganisms.

**Vermicomposting:** a managed system of converting food scraps into compost using earthworms. Many commercial vermicompost manufacturers use compost as a feed for their earthworms, breaking down the nitrogen in the biomatter and making it more bioavailable.

**Actively Aerated Compost Tea (AACT):** a dilution of compost in water actively aerated for twenty-four hours to ensure the microorganisms don't drown. Adding proteins such as fish hydrolysis helps boost fungi populations while adding carbs such as molasses increases bacterial populations.

**Mushroom compost:** a composting process that uses added synthetic nitrogen to speed the process up. Generally, only commercially available after it has been used to grow mushrooms but watch out for salt burn on your plants.

**Leaf mold:** not actually a compost per se, but a process that allows fungi to thrive. Because of the high lignin content in leaves, bacteria are poor decomposers, so fungi thrive. The product boosts the soil's water-holding capacity and nutrition levels. I add uric acid (urine) to increase the speed of the process from six months to six weeks.

## Aerobic Composting Elements

As the heading indicates, the differentiating need of the organisms involved in the aerobic composting process is air (oxygen). Below are the other essential conditions:

- Carbon-to-nitrogen ratio: A carbon-to-nitrogen ratio that can sustain microbial activity during the composting process is required. The carbon content must be sufficient to leave enough residual food to support continued biota activity once the compost is added to the soil.

- The management of temperature ranges: This is a balancing act between destroying pathogens and weed seeds in the mix without culling every member of the fungi family.

- The control of moisture content: To avoid anaerobic conditions, keep moisture levels below 60 percent.

- The distribution of active microorganisms throughout the process: This involves turning the pile and incorporating outer material into the inner high-activity arena.

- Managing available surface area for increased microbial activity, i.e., substrate particle size.

- The structure and composition of the compost pile: ensure your microorganisms don't suffocate while providing enough opportunity for heat and moisture distribution.

- Composting progress is influenced by both physical and chemical factors. Varying temperatures at different stages of the process are critical to composting success. Moisture content, air availability, ingredient particle size, and the nitrogen/carbon ratio affect decomposition rates. Additionally, the existing system's size, shape, and content affect aeration levels and the batch's ability to manage temperature levels.

- Soil is ultimately a biological system. When it comes to soil health, the goal should be to create a habitat that is ideal for microorganisms and macrofauna. Following this is a good starting point for creating a microorganism's breeding colony. [73] [74] [75] [76]

My compost bay is brimming with high-quality compost, meticulously prepared at Simplify Gardening. The rich, dark compost represents a valuable resource for nourishing plants and promoting vigorous growth in the garden.

### *Carbon*

Carbon is the primary food source for aerobic decomposition microorganisms. Some available carbon provides energy, and some is combined with nitrogen for cellular growth (body maintenance). The average microorganism's cell mass is approximately 88 percent carbon, and humans, in comparison, are 23 percent carbon. Microorganisms have an average C:N ratio of 8:1, something they need to maintain to stay alive—even in the soil.

While you may start your composting pile with the standard 30 parts of carbon to every nitrogen part (30:1), ending with a mere 10:1 ratio is typical (and ideal). In the composting process, some carbon dioxide is released during respiration. As a result, the carbon content of a compost pile is continuously decreasing, and the nitrogen portion is increasing. Not all weight reduction is due to carbon loss; some of the loss is in the form of water vapor. In the consumption of carbon, microorganisms produce heat, $CO_2$, water, and (thankfully) humus.

A starting ratio of 30 to 33:1 carbon to nitrogen is essential because:

- The lowest level of carbon suggested is 24:1. At that ratio, the microorganisms will consume all the carbon—two-thirds for energy and a third to maintain their cell structure. A lower carbon content would limit microbial population growth.

- If your carbon content is too high, the process initiation will be slow as the microbes need nitrogen for cellular growth and reproduction. Low organism populations mean a slow process.

- The C:N ratio must be reduced to a more appropriate level through several life cycles of organisms. Your final product will be carbon deficient if you have too much nitrogen (and limited carbon) in your raw material. Ammonia ($NH_3$) or ammonium ($NH_4^+$), both unstable forms of nitrogen, will form if protein decomposition is interrupted due to a lack of carbon. Toxic concentrations of gaseous ammonia or leaching nitrogen from the pile could contaminate nearby groundwater or surface waters.

- However, the C:N ratio does not always accurately reflect the number of nutrients available to microorganisms in compost. As mentioned earlier, bioavailability needs to be considered. Balancing the C:N ratio and bioavailability need consideration. Woody material bound by decay-resistant lignin is more difficult to decompose, whereas material containing simple sugars such as fruit waste decomposes quickly. Keratin is the only nitrogen source that is resistant to decay. Keratin is the fibrous protein tissue used in DNA testing—hair and nails. It also is found in the animal kingdom's horns, feathers, and wool.

### *Water*

As with all living creatures on Earth, microorganisms require water to live. Additionally, the mobility of these tiny creatures depends on a fluid-filled environment—for them and nutrients. Water also is the platform for chemical reactions.

The recommended moisture content for composting is between 40 and 65 percent. When the moisture content drops below 15 percent, all microorganisms hibernate. Evaporation and precipitation contribute to changes in the compost pile's moisture content during the composting process. Enough water and porosity must be constantly maintained during the process.

### *Oxygen*

Aerobic microorganisms cannot survive without oxygen. Anaerobic microbes take over the compost pile if adequate oxygen is not provided, slowing down the composting process.[77] This situation is most easily recognized by the foul odors released and can be remedied by adding some dry materials such as wood shavings. An oxygen concentration of 6 percent and above is required to maintain aerobic conditions.

### *Heat*

During the active composting period, the compost pile experiences a wide range of temperatures. Some microorganisms cannot survive when the temperature changes, while others thrive in new conditions. A home composting system has three temperature ranges during the active composting period, known as psychrophilic, mesophilic, and thermophilic, based on the types of prominent microorganisms in a pile at those temperatures.

Temperatures lower than 50°F (10°C) are considered psychrophilic. Psychrophilic organisms are most prevalent at the initiation of the process and during curing. The mesophilic organisms are active at temperatures between 50°F and 105°F (10°C and 40°C), while thermophilic microorganisms are responsible for temperatures above that and can reach temperatures high enough to ignite a dry batch. Ideally, we want to keep temperatures below 167°F (75°C) but occasionally above 155°F (68°C). These temperatures are generally achieved in the batch center first and should be closely monitored.

[top] The addition of straw into the compost mix provides an essential carbon source to balance the nitrogen-rich materials. This vital ingredient helps create the perfect environment for decomposing organisms, resulting in nutrient-rich compost for the garden.

[bottom] This compost pile is insulated with black plastic and carpet to regulate heat and moisture, speeding up decomposition for nutrient-rich compost.

The self-insulating compost traps heat generated by microbial activity as the population degrades the most readily degradable material and grows. As the microbial populations grow and diversify, the temperature increases steadily through the psychrophilic and mesophilic temperature ranges. Depending on the operation, compost piles can take anywhere from two to three days to transition from mesophilic activity to thermophilic (hot).

Depending on the process, the compost pile can stay in the thermophilic range for anywhere from ten to sixty days. Aerate the pile to reactivate active composting once the temperature drops below 105°F (40°C). Active composting is never determined to be finished at a specific point. When the pile conditions are such that microbial activity cannot increase enough to reheat the pile, it is usually considered complete and ready for curing.

## PLANT NUTRITION

A healthy and productive vegetable garden depends on the availability of twenty chemical elements that plants use for various functions. Plants get three of these elements from the air: carbon, hydrogen, and oxygen. The other seventeen elements come from the soil and are absorbed by the roots. These include nitrogen, phosphorus, potassium, calcium, magnesium, sulfur, iron, manganese, zinc, copper, boron, molybdenum, chlorine, nickel, cobalt, silicon, and sodium.

Some of these elements are needed in large amounts (macronutrients) and some in small amounts (micronutrients), but all are essential for plant growth. The soil's fertility depends on how well it can supply these elements to the plants. Too much or too little of any element can cause plant problems and affect their health and yield.

Nitrogen is one of the most important macronutrients for plants, but it can be harmful if applied excessively. Nitrogen is abundant in the air (78 percent of the atmosphere), but plants need it in a form they can use. Some plants (such as legumes), can fix nitrogen from the air with the help of bacteria in their roots but most plants rely on nitrogen from the soil.

Excess nitrogen can leach into groundwater and pose a health risk to humans, especially pregnant women. Therefore, gardeners should be careful not to overfertilize their plants with nitrogen. The best way to ensure that your plants get the right amount and balance of nutrients is to test your soil regularly and amend it with organic matter and fertilizers as needed. Organic matter can improve the soil's structure, water retention, and microbial activity, and provide some nutrients to the plants. Fertilizers can supplement the soil's natural fertility and correct deficiencies or imbalances.

## SOIL FERTILITY

Soil fertility is the ability of soil to provide nutrients and water for plant growth and development. It depends on various factors, such as soil texture, structure, organic

## The Importance of Curing Compost

Even though microbial activity becomes insufficient to raise temperatures, your batch is still in a process of carbon degradation. Keeping it slightly damp while it's in storage for a further six weeks will ensure a more complete carbon decomposition. This is important because if the organic matter content is too high, the organisms will immobilize nitrogen in your soil when you add the compost, using the soil's nitrogen to complete the job.

Nitrogen availability to plants is briefly decreased during immobilization. To metabolize the remaining carbon, bacteria require extra nitrogen. Protein synthesis is inhibited when growing microorganisms utilize the $NO_3^-$-N and/or $NH_4^+$-N already present in the soil. When uncured compost is added to beds, the actively growing microorganism populations immobilize some of the soil's nitrogen. The consumed nitrogen will become available to plants later, so it is prudent to add compost to beds a month before the beds will be used for growing plants.

matter, pH, cation exchange capacity (CEC), microbial activity, and nutrient availability. Soil fertility can be improved by adding organic or inorganic fertilizers, compost, manure, crop rotation, cover crops, mulching, and conservation tillage. Soil fertility is compromised by erosion, compaction, salinization, acidification, pollution, and overuse of chemical inputs.

# Some of the Essential Plant Nutrients

**Nitrogen (N):** Nitrogen is the most limiting nutrient for plant growth and is a part of proteins, enzymes, chlorophyll, and nucleic acids. Nitrogen can be sourced from the atmosphere by nitrogen-fixing bacteria or from the soil by nitrification and mineralization of organic matter. Nitrogen is available to plants in two inorganic forms: ammonium ($NH_4^+$) and nitrate ($NO_3^-$).

**Phosphorus (P):** Phosphorus is essential for energy transfer, nucleic acid synthesis, root development, and seed formation. Phosphorus is sourced mainly from the soil by dissolving primary and secondary minerals or mineralizing organic matter. Phosphorus is available to plants in two inorganic forms: orthophosphate ($H_2PO_4^-$ and $HPO_4^{2-}$) and polyphosphate ($PO_4^{3-}$).

**Potassium (K):** Potassium is involved in enzyme activation, osmoregulation, stomatal movement, photosynthesis, and translocation of sugars. Potassium is sourced mainly from the soil by weathering primary minerals or by release from clay minerals and organic matter. Potassium is available to plants in one inorganic form: potassium ion ($K^+$).

**Calcium (Ca):** Calcium is essential for cell wall formation, membrane stability, cell division, and signaling. Calcium is sourced mainly from the soil by dissolving primary and secondary minerals or by exchange with soil cations. Calcium is available to plants in one inorganic form: calcium ion ($Ca_2^+$).

**Magnesium (Mg):** Magnesium is a central component of chlorophyll and is involved in enzyme activation, protein synthesis, and phosphate metabolism. Magnesium is sourced mainly from the soil by dissolution of primary and secondary minerals or by exchange with soil cations. Magnesium is available to plants in one inorganic form: magnesium ion ($Mg_2^+$).

**Sulfur (S):** Sulfur is a constituent of amino acids, proteins, coenzymes, vitamins, and secondary metabolites. Sulfur can be sourced from the atmosphere by the deposition of sulfur dioxide or from the soil by oxidation of sulfides or reduction of sulfates. Sulfur is available to plants in two inorganic forms: sulfate ($SO_4^{2-}$) and sulfide ($S_2^-$).

**Iron (Fe):** Iron is a cofactor of many enzymes involved in electron transport, nitrogen fixation, chlorophyll synthesis, and oxygen transport. Iron is sourced mainly from the soil by reducing ferric iron ($Fe_3^+$) to ferrous iron ($Fe_2+$) or by chelation with organic acids or siderophores.

**Manganese (Mn):** Manganese is a cofactor of many enzymes involved in photosynthesis, respiration, nitrogen metabolism, and synthesis of phenolic compounds. Manganese is sourced mainly from the soil by reducing manganese dioxide ($MnO_2$) to manganous ion ($Mn_2^+$) or by chelation with organic acids.

**Zinc (Zn):** Zinc is a cofactor of many enzymes involved in protein synthesis, auxin metabolism, and membrane stability. Zinc is sourced mainly from the soil by dissolution of primary and secondary minerals or by chelation with organic acids or phytosiderophores. Zinc is available to plants in one inorganic form: zinc ion ($Zn_2^+$).

**Chlorine (Cl):** Chlorine is an essential plant micronutrient that participates in several physiological processes. Plants take chlorine as the soil solution's chloride ($Cl^-$) anion. Chloride is involved in splitting water to produce oxygen during photosynthesis, controlling osmosis and turgor pressure, regulating the opening and closing of stomata, and enhancing disease resistance and tolerance.

**Copper (Cu):** Copper is a cofactor of many enzymes involved in electron transport, lignin synthesis, hormone perception, and oxidative stress response. Copper is sourced mainly from the soil by dissolution of primary and secondary minerals or by chelation with organic acids or phytosiderophores. Copper is available to plants in two inorganic forms: cuprous ion ($Cu^+$) and cupric ion ($Cu_2^+$).

**Boron (B):** Boron is an essential plant micronutrient, but often it is deficient in soils. Plants mainly use boron as boric acid, the predominant form in soil solution at neutral or slightly acidic pH. Boron is essential for plant health because it is involved in cell wall formation, membrane stability, sugar transport, pollen tube growth, and seed development.

**Molybdenum (Mo):** Molybdenum is a plant micronutrient essential for nitrogen fixation and nitrate reduction. It is available to plants as molybdate ($MoO_4^{2-}$), which is taken up by the roots from the soil solution. Molybdenum synthesizes and activates several enzymes that regulate plant growth and development, such as nitrate reductase, nitrogenase, and sulfite oxidase. Molybdenum deficiency can cause chlorosis, stunting, and poor flowering and fruiting in plants.

## Fertilizer and the Environment

Field runoff of natural and synthetic nitrogen and phosphorus can contaminate water supplies and boost greenhouse gas emissions, both of which contribute to global warming. Gardeners can reduce their negative effects on the environment and maximize the effectiveness of their fertilizer use with some careful planning. Splitting nitrogen additions to smaller more frequent applications is more effective (and safer) than bigger, less frequent applications.

Broadcasting all phosphorus is typically less effective than banding it at planting. Because phosphorus is not easily transported through soil, it is advised to be applied as a side-dressing. Gardeners don't need to worry too much about potash and the macronutrients polluting the groundwater, but they still need to be managed effectively to cut costs and maximize yields.

As you can see, balancing soil health and plant nutrition needs is critical to the success of any vegetable garden. Understanding how nutrients affect plant growth in different ways is key to maintaining optimum plant nutrition in your plot. Next, let's take a look at the various plant families typically grown in a home garden and discuss how their care needs are similar within each group, and how gardeners who understand their collective management needs can grow a healthier, more productive edible garden.

Thoughtful fertilization preserves soil life and provides your plants with the nutrients they need.

My impressive rhubarb plants, towering more than 5 feet (1.5 m) tall.

# Chapter 6:

## Vegetable Gardening Groups

Vegetables can be grouped by their hardiness to cold, subdivided into warm- and cool-season plants, or grouped per botanical family. Another grouping, known as the EPA grouping, is based on their management needs. It can all become quite complex, but my goal is to simplify gardening. While knowing the different families is helpful, what we're really interested in is optimizing plant productivity and managing risks. The goal of the EPA is to prevent the abuse of herbicides and pesticides as applied to managing plant pathogens and counter-productive plant species. Plants that share common features share common risks. Risks also are shared by plant family groups.

In this chapter we explore the specifics of these plant groupings, including hardiness factors, the management approaches they share, and the nutritional guidelines to balance environmental health, plant productivity, and product quality. Rather than cover each individual plant's specific growing needs (e.g., planting depth, optimal soil temperature, etc.), we're covering the principles behind entire plant groups, including their shared needs and potential risks. My goal is to enhance your general gardening competence, not teach you how to paint-by-numbers. So, let's explore the groups.

*PS. All fertilization, yield, and watering tables are standardized to beds that are 10 feet long × 4 feet wide (3 meters long × 1.2 meters wide for readers using the metric system).*

| Vegetable Plant Family Groups | | |
| --- | --- | --- |
| **Scientific Name** | **Common Family Name** | **Crops** |
| Amaranthaceae | Amaranth Family | Amaranth, Beet, Lamb's-quarters, Quinoa, Spinach, Swiss Chard |
| Amaryllidaceae | Allium Family | Chives, Garlic, Leeks, Onions, Scallions, Shallots |
| Apiaceae | Carrot or Parsley Family | Angelica, Anise, Caraway, Carrot, Celery, Coriander, Cumin, Dill, Fennel, Lovage, Parsley, Parsnip |
| Asteraceae | Composite Family | Artichoke, Chicory, Dandelion, Endive, Escarole, Lettuce, Sunflower |
| Brassicaceae | Mustard Family | Broccoli, Brussels Sprouts, Cabbage, Cauliflower, Collards, Kale, Kohlrabi, Mustard, Radishes, Rutabaga, Turnip |
| Convolvulaceae | Bindweed Family | Sweet potato |
| Cucurbitaceae | Gourd Family | Cucumbers, Gourds, Melons, Pumpkins, Squashes (Summer), Squashes (Winter), Watermelon |
| Dioscoreaceae | Yam Family | Yams |
| Euphorbiaceae | Cassava Family | Cassava |
| Fabaceae | Pea Family | Beans, Chickpeas, Fava Beans, Lentils, Lima Beans, Peas, Soybeans |
| Lamiaceae | Mint/Herb Family | Basil, Hyssop, Lavender, Marjoram, Mint, Oregano, Perilla, Rosemary, Sage, Savory, Thyme |
| Malvaceae | Mallow Family | Okra |
| Musaceae | Banana Family | Plantain |
| Poaceae | Grass Family | Barley, Corn, Pearl Millet, Oats, Rye, Sweet Corn, Wheat |
| Polygonaceae | Buckwheat/Petiole Family | Rhubarb |
| Solanaceae | Nightshade Family | Eggplant, Pepper, Potato, Tomato |

## EPA Grouping

The Code of Federal Regulations in the Pesticide Programs, Tolerances and Exemptions for Pesticide Chemical Residues in Food Section, Crop Group Tables (Title-40, Chapter I, Subchapter E, Part 180, Subpart B, Section 180.41) lists the following vegetable groups (among others that most home gardeners do not grow).[78]

| Plant Risk Management Groups | |
|---|---|
| **EPA Crop Group** | **Crops** |
| Group 1: Root and Tuber Vegetables | Beet, Carrot, Celeriac, Turnip, Chicory, Ginseng, Horseradish, Parsnip, Radish, Rutabaga, Salsify, Artichoke, Cassava, Ginger, Potato, Sweet Potato, Turmeric, Yam |
| Group 3: Bulb Vegetables | Garlic, Leek, Onion, Shallot, Chive |
| Group 4: Leafy Greens and Leafy Petioles | Arugula (Rocket), Broccoli, Raab Cabbage, Chinese Cabbage, Bok Choy, Cabbage, Collards, Cress, Garden Cress, Kale, Mustard Greens, Rape Greens, Shepherd's Purse, Watercress |
| Group 5: Cole Crops and Brassica Leafy Greens | Broccoli, Brussels Sprouts, Cabbage, Cauliflower, Kale, Kohlrabi, Mustard Greens, Turnip Greens |
| Group 6: Legume Vegetables | Beans, Peas, Southern Peas/Cowpeas, Lima Beans |
| Group 8: Fruiting Vegetables | Eggplant, Pepper, Okra, Tomato |
| Group 9: Cucurbit Vegetables | Cantaloupe/Muskmelon, Cucumber, Pumpkin, Squash, Watermelon |
| Group 15: Cereal Grains | Barley, Buckwheat, Corn, Millet, Oats, Popcorn, Rice, Rye, Sorghum, Wheat |
| Group 19: Herbs and Spices | Basil, Cilantro (Coriander), Dill, Fennel, Florence Fennel, Lavender, Marjoram, Oregano, Parsley, Rosemary, Sage, Savory, Tarragon, Thyme |
| Group 20: Oilseeds | Calendula, Castor Oil Plant, Euphorbia, Evening Primrose, Jojoba, Safflower, Sunflower |
| Group 22: Stalk, Stem, and Leaf Petiole Vegetables | Agave, Aloe Vera, Asparagus, Bamboo Shoots, Prickly Pear |
| Group 25: Herbs | Basil, Bay, Borage, Mint, Oregano, Sage, Sorrel, Thyme, and hundreds more. |

These groups make managing plants easier by grouping plants with similar risk-mitigation needs together. Here is the summarized list for home garden crops:

- Group 1—Root and Tuber Vegetables
- Group 3—Bulb Vegetables
- Group 4—Leafy Greens and Leafy Petioles
- Group 5—Cole Crops and Brassica Leafy Greens
- Group 6—Legume Vegetables
- Group 8—Fruiting Vegetables
- Group 9—Cucurbit Vegetables
- Group 15—Cereal Grains
- Group 19—Herbs and Spices
- Group 20—Oilseeds
- Group 22—Stalk, Stem, and Leaf Petiole Vegetables
- Group 25—Herbs

## Plant Hardiness Groups

The list below is ordered according to hardiness based on the plant's preferred soil temperature. Please note that this temperature should be taken at a depth of 4 inches (10 cm).

| Preferred Soil Temperatures | | | | | |
|---|---|---|---|---|---|
| Plant | Growth Season | Ideal Soil Temperature | Germination Range | EPA Group | Plant Family |
| Spinach | Cool | 60°F (16°C) | 40°F–75°F (~4°C–24°C) | 4 | Amaranthaceae |
| Kale | Cool | 60°F (16°C) | 45°F–85°F (~7°C–30°C) | 5 | Brassicaceae |
| Mustard | Cool | 60°F (16°C) | 45°F–85°F (~7°C–30°C) | 5 | Brassicaceae |
| Rutabaga | Cool | 60°F (16°C) | 45°F–85°F (~7°C–30°C) | 5 | Brassicaceae |
| Turnip | Cool | 60°F (16°C) | 45°F–85°F (~7°C–30°C) | 5 | Brassicaceae |
| Bok Choy | Cool | 65°F (18°C) | 50°F–80°F (~10°C–27°C) | 5 | Brassicaceae |
| Swiss Chard | Cool | 70°F (21°C) | 50°F–85°F (~10°C–30°C) | 4 | Amaranthaceae |
| Lettuce | Cool | 70°F (21°C) | 45°F–85°F (~7°C–30°C) | 4 | Asteraceae |
| Beets | Cool | 70°F (21°C) | 50°F–85°F (~10°C–30°C) | 1 | Amaranthaceae |
| Onions | Cool | 72°F (22°C) | 45°F–85°F (~7°C–30°C) | 3 | Amaryllidaceae |
| Scallions | Cool | 72°F (22°C) | 45°F–95°F (~7°C–35°C) | 3 | Amaryllidaceae |
| Shallots | Cool | 72°F (22°C) | 45°F–95°F (~7°C–35°C) | 3 | Amaryllidaceae |
| Celery | Cool | 72°F (22°C) | 70°F–75°F (~21°C–24°C) | 4 | Apiaceae |

## Preferred Soil Temperatures

| Plant | Growth Season | Ideal Soil Temperature | Germination Range | EPA Group | Plant Family |
|---|---|---|---|---|---|
| Endive | Cool | 75°F (24°C) | 45°F–85°F (~7°C–30°C) | 4 | Asteraceae |
| Potato | Warm | 75°F (24°C) | 42°F–85°F (~6°C–30°C) | 1 | Solanaceae |
| Peas | Warm | 75°F (24°C) | 60°F–85°F (~16°C–30°C) | 6 | Fabaceae |
| Broccoli | Cool | 77°F (25°C) | 45°F–85°F (~7°C–30°C) | 5 | Brassicaceae |
| Brussels Sprouts | Cool | 77°F (25°C) | 45°F–85°F (~7°C–30°C) | 5 | Brassicaceae |
| Cabbage | Cool | 77°F (25°C) | 45°F–85°F (~7°C–30°C) | 5 | Brassicaceae |
| Cauliflower | Cool | 77°F (25°C) | 45°F–85°F (~7°C–30°C) | 5 | Brassicaceae |
| Collard Greens | Cool | 77°F (25°C) | 45°F–85°F (~7°C–30°C) | 5 | Brassicaceae |
| Kohlrabi | Cool | 77°F (25°C) | 45°F–85°F (~7°C–30°C) | 5 | Brassicaceae |
| Chives | Cool | 77°F (25°C) | 45°F–95°F (~7°C–35°C) | 3 | Amaryllidaceae |
| Leeks | Cool | 77°F (25°C) | 45°F–95°F (~7°C–35°C) | 3 | Amaryllidaceae |
| Parsnip | Cool | 77°F (25°C) | 50°F–85°F (~10°C–30°C) | 1 | Apiaceae |
| Radishes | Cool | 77°F (25°C) | 55°F–85°F (~13°C–30°C) | 1 | Brassicaceae |
| Corn (Sweet) | Warm | 77°F (25°C) | 65°F–85°F (~18°C–30°C) | 15 | Poaceae |
| Beans | Warm | 77°F (25°C) | 70°F–80°F (~21°C–27°C) | 6 | Fabaceae |
| Lima Beans | Warm | 77°F (25°C) | 70°F–80°F (~21°C–27°C) | 6 | Fabaceae |
| Soybean | Warm | 77°F (25°C) | 70°F–80°F (~21°C–27°C) | 6 | Fabaceae |
| Carrots | Cool | 80°F (27°C) | 50°F–85°F (~10°C–30°C) | 1 | Apiaceae |
| Tomato | Warm | 82°F (28°C) | 60°F–95°F (~16°C–35°C) | 8 | Solanaceae |
| Cucumber | Warm | 85°F (30°C) | 60°F–90°F (~16°C–32°C) | 9 | Cucurbitaceae |
| Eggplant | Warm | 85°F (30°C) | 60°F–95°F (~16°C–35°C) | 8 | Solanaceae |
| Gourds | Warm | 85°F (30°C) | 60°F–95°F (~16°C–35°C) | 9 | Cucurbitaceae |
| Melons | Warm | 85°F (30°C) | 60°F–95°F (~16°C–35°C) | 9 | Cucurbitaceae |
| Pumpkin | Warm | 85°F (30°C) | 60°F–95°F (~16°C–35°C) | 9 | Cucurbitaceae |
| Squash | Warm | 85°F (30°C) | 60°F–95°F (~16°C–35°C) | 9 | Cucurbitaceae |
| Peppers | Warm | 85°F (30°C) | 70°F–95°F (~21°C–35°C) | 8 | Solanaceae |
| Watermelon | Warm | 85°F (30°C) | 70°F–95°F (~21°C–35°C) | 9 | Cucurbitaceae |

# AMARANTH FAMILY (*AMARANTHACEAE*)

| Common Name | Botanical Name | Management Approach (EPA) |
|---|---|---|
| Amaranth | *Amaranthus* | Group 4: Leafy Greens and Leafy Petioles |
| Beets | *Beta vulgaris* | Group 1: Root and Tuber Vegetables |
| Swiss Chard | *Beta vulgaris* ssp. *cicla* | Group 4: Leafy Greens and Leafy Petioles |
| Lamb's-quarters | *Chenopodium album* | Group 4: Leafy Greens and Leafy Petioles |
| Quinoa | *Chenopodium quinoa* | Group 15: Cereal Grains |
| Spinach | *Spinacia oleracea* | Group 4: Leafy Greens and Leafy Petioles |

## Overview

### *Beets*

Beet is a root vegetable cultivated for its edible roots and leaves, which are rich in vitamins, minerals, antioxidants, and dietary fiber. Beet can grow in various climates and soil types, but it prefers cool weather and moist, well-drained soil.

Beet seeds can be sown directly in the garden or started indoors and transplanted later. Beet plants need regular watering and weeding to prevent diseases and pests. Beets can be harvested when they reach the desired size, usually between fifty and seventy days after planting. Beet leaves can be harvested throughout the growing season as a fresh or cooked green.

Swiss chard is a leafy green vegetable rich in vitamins, minerals, and antioxidants, and can be eaten raw or cooked. It is easy to grow in most climates, as it tolerates both cold and heat well. It can be planted in early spring or late summer, and harvested throughout the growing season.

Swiss chard prefers well-drained soil with plenty of organic matter and a sunny or partially shaded location.

This bed of young beet plants is growing vibrantly and the plants are evenly spaced. The healthy green foliage indicates that they are well-nurtured and thriving, a testament to diligent garden care and proper soil preparation.

It can be grown in containers, raised beds, or in-ground gardens. Swiss chard can be harvested by cutting the outer leaves at the base, leaving the inner leaves to grow back. Alternatively, the whole plant can be pulled up when it reaches maturity.

Spinach can be planted in early spring or fall, depending on the climate. Spinach likes cool weather and moist, well-drained soil with a neutral pH. Seeds can be sown directly into the soil as soon as the ground is workable, about ½ inch (12 mm) deep and 2 inches (5 cm) apart.

Spinach plants should be thinned to 3 to 4 inches (8 to 10 cm) apart when they have their first true leaves. Spinach can be harvested in as little as one month after planting, by cutting the outer leaves or the whole plant. Spinach is rich in iron, calcium, and vitamins A, B, and C, and can be eaten raw or cooked.

### Amaranthaceae Fertilizer Recommendations

Maintain a soil pH of 6.5 to 6.8 for leafy greens. Pay special attention to spinach; it is particularly sensitive to acidity. Do not exceed recommendations and subtract any nitrogen values that might be soilborne due to organic matter and legume cover crops. Start with less and respond to your plant's needs. Distributed feeding is better than occasional bulk feeding, unless you are boosting base in-soil fertility before planting, as informed by current valid soil-test results. Phosphorus and potassium quantities as well and the nitrogen starter are added to the soil before planting. In the table below the imperial amounts are for a 40-square foot bed (10 × 4 ft) and the metric amounts are for a 3.6-meter (3 × 1.2 m) bed.

[top] The captivating beauty of Swiss chard, features bright, vivid stems in an array of colors, contrasted against lush green leaves. The healthy appearance and vibrant display make it a striking addition to any garden, providing nutritional value and visual appeal.

[bottom] Bright green spinach leaves thrive in the garden. The lush and healthy leaves are a testament to the quality of care they receive. They add visual appeal to the garden, and they are a nutritious and versatile addition to any meal.

| Recommended NPK Fertilizers | | | | | | | | | |
|---|---|---|---|---|---|---|---|---|---|
| Crop | N Starter | | N Side-dressings | | Phosphorus (P) | | Potassium (K) | |
| Beets | 0.73 oz | 20.18 g | 0.44 oz | 12.11 g | 1.47 oz | 40.35 g | 1.47 oz | 40.35 g |
| Spinach | 0.88 oz | 24.21 g | 0.44 oz | 12.11 g | 2.20 oz | 60.53 g | 2.20 oz | 60.53 g |
| Swiss Chard | 0.73 oz | 20.18 g | 0.44 oz | 12.11 g | 1.47 oz | 40.35 g | 1.47 oz | 40.35 g |

## Mitigating Root and Tuber Vegetable Risks (Group 1)

Plants included in the root and tuber vegetable group are beet, carrot, horseradish, parsnip, potato, radish, rutabaga, sweet potato, turnip, yams. Note that these risks extend to plants beyond the Amaranthaceae family (beet) to include some plants from the Apiaceae (carrot and parsnip), Brassicaceae (horseradish, radish, rutabaga, and turnip), Convolvulaceae (sweet potato), Dioscoreaceae (yam), and Solanaceae (potato) families.

## *Pests Common to Root and Tuber Vegetable Crops*

Aphids, carrot weevil beetles, caterpillars (cutworms), flea beetles, leafhoppers, and seed and root maggots are common pests you'll need to pay attention to.

Please note that not all pesticides for a specific pest can be used on all plants. Some insecticides are pest and plant specific. It is beyond the scope of this book to offer pesticide advice, but most Extension offices have great resources, and some excellent region-specific collaboration work can be found at VegetableGrowersNews.com.[81]

| Common Diseases | | |
|---|---|---|
| **Disease** | **Pathogen** | **Prevention** |
| Aster Yellows (Purple-top Wilt) | Phytoplasma mollicutes | • Remove infected plants.<br>• Manage leafhoppers.<br>• Ensure seed hygiene. |
| Brittle Root (horseradish) | *Spiroplasma citri* bacteria | • Manage leafhoppers. |
| Cavity Spot (carrots) | *Pythium oomycetes* | • Ensure general hygiene.<br>• Use warmer water, 68°F to 77°F (20°C to 25°C).<br>• Improve drainage. |
| Damping-off Seed and Seedling Rots | Various pathogens, including *Fusarium* spp. and *Pythium* spp. | • Ensure general hygiene.<br>• Use warmer water, 68°F to 77°F (20°C to 25°C) when watering.<br>• Improve drainage. |
| Root Discoloration (horseradish) | *Fusarium* and *Verticillium* fungi | • Use disease-free rootstocks.<br>• Root hygiene using hot water treatment: 115°F (46°C) for 10 minutes. |
| Leaf Blight | *Xanthomonas* bacteria and *Alternaria* fungus | • Use disease-free seed.<br>• Ensure seed hygiene.<br>• Use crop rotation.<br>• Promptly rogue finished crops to prevent disease buildup. |
| Leaf Spot | *Cercospora* fungus, *Ramularia cynarae* | • Use disease-free seed.<br>• Ensure seed hygiene.<br>• Use crop rotation.<br>• Promptly rogue finished crops to prevent disease buildup. |
| Nematodes | Several nematode species | • Proliferation of beneficial microorganisms by compost additions.<br>• Anaerobic soil disinfestation (ASD) is an effective soil sterilization method.<br>• Promptly rogue finished crops to prevent disease buildup. |
| Viruses | Several species | • Manage aphid populations as they spread viruses.<br>• Ensure starter health (root or tuber). |
| White Rust | *Albugo* oomycete | • Seed hygiene: 122°F (50°C) for 25 minutes.<br>• Use crop rotation.<br>• Ensure adequate airflow and drainage (raised beds). |

# ALLIUM FAMILY (*AMARYLLIDACEAE*)

| Common Name | Botanical Name | Management Approach (EPA) |
|---|---|---|
| Chives | *Allium schoenoprasum* | Group 3: Bulb Vegetables |
| Garlic | *Allium sativum* | Group 3: Bulb Vegetables |
| Leeks | *Allium ampeloprasum var. porrum* | Group 3: Bulb Vegetables |
| Onions | *Allium cepa* | Group 3: Bulb Vegetables |
| Scallions | *Allium cepa* | Group 3: Bulb Vegetables |
| Shallots | *Allium cepa var. aggregatum* | Group 3: Bulb Vegetables |

## Managing Bulb Vegetables

Several vegetables and herbs, including onions, leeks, chives, and garlic, can be used to give dishes a bolder taste. They mimic the appearance of root vegetables but are something else entirely. Leaves or swelling stems are the harvested and consumed pieces. While onions and leeks only live for two years, their other related species typically live for much longer. Some can survive in the ground for a long time, such chives and Egyptian walking onions. Still others are gathered when the season is over. A portion of the stem (the garlic clove, for instance) is kept for replanting the following year.

## Fertilizer Recommendations for Bulb Vegetables

Maintain a soil pH of 6.0 to 6.8, more acidic if your soil is rich in organic material.

If planting on organic soils with a pH over 6.0, include 0.16 ounces of manganese sulfate per 10-foot row (4.36 g per 3-m row) in the starter band. Side-dress bulb onions with 1.4 ounces per 10-foot bed (38.33 g per 3-m bed) in mid-June or split that amount between early and late June.

Reduce the amount of nitrogen added by the value of credits from previously grown legume crops, animal manures and compost, and soils with more than 3 percent organic matter. NPK quantities for different bulb and crown crops are listed on the following page, and the imperial amounts are for a 40-square foot bed (10 × 4 ft) and the metric amounts are for a 3.6-meter bed (3 × 1.2 m). Do not apply nitrogen once bulbs have started forming—will avoid several diseases.

## Recommended NPK fertilizers

| Crop | N Starter | | N Side-dressings | | Phosphorus (P) | | Potassium (K) | |
|---|---|---|---|---|---|---|---|---|
| Garlic | 1.10 oz | 30.26 g | 0.73 oz | 20.18 g | 2.20 oz | 60.53 g | 2.20 oz | 60.53 g |
| Green Onions | 0.88 oz | 24.21 g | 0.73 oz | 20.18 g | 1.47 oz | 40.35 g | 1.47 oz | 40.35 g |
| Leek | 0.88 oz | 24.21 g | 0.44 oz | 12.11 g | 2.20 oz | 60.53 g | 2.20 oz | 60.53 g |
| Onion Bulbs | 0.88 oz | 24.21 g | 0.44 oz | 12.11 g | 1.47 oz | 40.35 g | 1.47 oz | 40.35 g |

## Growing Asparagus

Asparagus isn't an allium, but for a long time both were in the same family (Liliaceae). Now asparagus is in its own family, Asparagaceae, and allium is in Amaryllidaceae. Since they are treated similarly, asparagus has been included here.

Asparagus is generally managed as a Group 22: Stalk, Stem, and Leaf Petiole Vegetable, along with agave, bamboo shoots, Aloe vera, and others.

Note the additional potassium (K) that asparagus needs in the fertilizer chart below.

By meticulously planting asparagus crowns in my garden, I can ensure the plants have the best possible start, leading to a bountiful harvest in the coming seasons.

| Common Name | Botanical Name | Management Approach (EPA) |
|---|---|---|
| Asparagus | *Asparagus officinalis* | Group 22: Stalk, Stem, and Leaf Petiole Vegetable |

## Recommended NPK fertilizers

| Crop | N Starter | | N Side-dressings | | Phosphorus (P) | | Potassium (K) | |
|---|---|---|---|---|---|---|---|---|
| Asparagus | 0.73 oz | 20.18 g | 0.73 oz | 20.18 g | 2.20 oz | 60.53 g | 3.31 oz | 90.79 g |

## Mitigating Bulb Vegetable Risks (Group 3)

### *Common Pests*

Other than seed and root maggots, onions and related crops have very few pest problems.

[top right] This close-up photo reveals a root maggot, an unwanted pest that can cause damage to bulbous plants such as alliums. Its presence serves as a reminder for gardeners to remain vigilant and practice proper pest control measures to protect their crops.

[bottom right] Onions, chives, garlic, shallots, and other members of the onion family are great additions to the garden.

| Common Diseases | | |
|---|---|---|
| **Disease** | **Pathogen** | **Prevention** |
| Fusarium Basal Rot | *Fusarium oxysporum* f. sp. *cepae* | • Plant resistant cultivars.<br>• Use crop rotation—avoiding beds with a Fusarium basal rot history.<br>• Increase beneficial microbes by compost addition.<br>• Manage soil insects and foliar diseases.<br>• Use bulbs stored at temperatures below 40°F (4°C) and at humidity rates of about 70 percent. |
| Damping-off Seed and Seedling Rots | Various pathogens, including *Fusarium* spp. and *Pythium* spp. | • Ensure general hygiene.<br>• Use warmer water, 68°F to 77°F (20°C to 25°C).<br>• Improve drainage. |
| Downy Mildew | *Peronospora* oomycete | • Improve soil drainage.<br>• Rotate crops.<br>• Avoid excessive humidity, leaf-wetting, and waterlogged soil.<br>• Ensure seed and set hygiene. |
| Gray Mold | *Botrytis* fungus | • Maintain effective post-crop hygiene.<br>• Ensure adequate airflow (plant spacing).<br>• Remove infected plants. |
| Leaf Blight and Center Rot | *Pantoea* bacteria | • Ensure effective post-crop hygiene.<br>• Warm, humid, and wet weather favors outbreaks, so manage drainage and airflow (plant spacing).<br>• Remove infected plants. |

(chart continues on page 134)

| Common Diseases | | |
|---|---|---|
| **Disease** | **Pathogen** | **Prevention** |
| Leaf Blight and Stalk Rot | *Stemphylium vesicarium* fungus | • Ensure effective post-crop hygiene.<br>• Ensure adequate airflow (plant spacing).<br>• Remove infected plants. |
| Leaf Blight | *Botrytis* fungus,<br>*Xanthomonas* bacteria | • Use disease-free seeds and sets.<br>• Rotate to non-host crops for three to four years.<br>• Monitor thrips populations.<br>• Ensure prompt destruction of the finished crop and cull piles. |
| Leaf Streak | *Pseudomonas viridiflava* | • Clip leaves when neck is dry.<br>• Manage nitrogen excesses.<br>• Employ good harvesting practices.<br>• Ensure crop hygiene. |
| Botrytis Neck Rot | *Botrytis aclada* and *B. allii* | • Post-harvest storage disease.<br>• Ensure crop hygiene.<br>• Destroy infected crop or stock to prevent spores spreading for miles on the wind.<br>• Harvest only mature, well-cored bulbs.<br>• Manage humidity post-harvest (max 70 percent). |
| Pink Root | *Phoma* fungus | • Use of resistant varieties.<br>• Maintain healthy plants with optimum fertility.<br>• Ensure crop hygiene.<br>• Don't rotate with cereal crops. |
| Purple Blotch | *Alternaria* fungus | • Use disease-free seeds and sets.<br>• Rotate to non-host crops for three to four years.<br>• Monitor thrips populations.<br>• Destroy the finished crop and cull piles promptly. |
| Slippery Skin and Sour Rot | *Burkholderia* bacteria | • Onions should be harvested when the bulbs have reached full maturity and should not be stored until they have been properly dried.<br>• Minimizing stem and bulb injury and avoiding overhead irrigation when the crop is approaching maturity can reduce losses from this disease. |
| Smut | *Urocystis* fungus | • Use disease-free seed and sets.<br>• Plant in areas with adequate drainage and air movement to reduce leaf wetness and humidity.<br>• Rotate to non-host crop for three years.<br>• Avoid late-season fertilizer applications or overhead irrigation. |
| White Rot | *Stromatinia cepivorum* or *Sclerotinia sclerotiorum* fungi | • Ensure crop hygiene.<br>• Plant only clean stock from known origins.<br>• Irrigation reduction will limit damage.<br>• Do not compost infected plants. |

# PARSLEY FAMILY (*APIACEAE*)

| Common Name | Botanical Name | Management Approach (EPA) |
| --- | --- | --- |
| Angelica | *Angelica archangelica* | Group 19: Herbs and Spices |
| Anise | *Pimpinella anisum* | Group 19: Herbs and Spices |
| Caraway | *Carum carvi* | Group 19: Herbs and Spices |
| Carrot | *Daucus carota* ssp. *sativus* | Group 1: Root and Tuber Vegetables |
| Celery | *Apium graveolens* | Group 4: Leafy Greens and Leafy Petioles |
| Coriander | *Coriandrum sativum* | Group 19: Herbs and Spices |
| Cumin | *Cuminum cyminum* | Group 19: Herbs and Spices |
| Dill | *Anethum graveolens* | Group 19: Herbs and Spices |
| Fennel | *Foeniculum vulgare* | Group 19: Herbs and Spices |
| Lovage | *Levisticum officinale* | Group 19: Herbs and Spices |
| Parsley | *Petroselinum crispum* | Group 4: Leafy Greens and Leafy Petioles |
| Parsnip | *Pastinaca sativa* | Group 1: Root and Tuber Vegetables |

I enjoy planting a variety of herbs in a beautifully crafted stone raised bed, creating a substantial and thriving herb garden to enhance any meal.

The Apiaceae are a diverse group of plants that includes herbs, spices, ornamentals, and vegetables. Several members of the family are a source of compounds that have medicinal and industrial applications. Dill is used as a biopesticide, and caraway is used in agriculture as an antifungal agent and insect repellent. Sometimes referred to by the former name Umbelliferae, the Apiaceae family consists of about 434 genera and nearly 3,780 species of plants mainly found in temperate regions. Just remember that while carrots and parsnip do better with fresh seeds, celery seeds do better the older they are—between three and five years. For leafy vegetables, maintain a soil pH of 6.5 to 6.8, and 6.0 to 7.0 for herbs.

[top] Carrots are among the most popular members of the Apiaceae family. There are many types of carrots you can grow in a home garden.

[bottom] Parlsey is a great plant for growing in cold frames as it is a very cold-tolerant biennial that produces delicious leafy greens.

## Managing Leafy Vegetables and Herbs

The herbs in this family are all similar, and leaf-sizes should guide you in the amount of sun they get. Small leaves need full sun, and larger leaves will manage some shade. They're all cool-season plants that need longer growing seasons. Avoid extended exposure to temperatures below 50°F (10°C) and above 75°F (24°C). Soil temperatures should be in the lower 70s°F (21°C to 24°C). Soil can be slightly acidic (pH between 6.0 and 6.8), and all of them, except the Angelica, do well in pots.

Keep the soil consistently moist, ensuring the bed or pot drains well. A mix of 30 percent compost, 30 percent inert materials such as pumice or perlite, and 40 percent peat moss should be ideal for pots. I generally advise using coconut coir, but the peat moss will help boost the needed acidity in this case.

The whole Apiaceae family attract beneficial insects. Be careful of confusing *Angelica archangelica* with the similar *Conium maculatum* (poison hemlock) which is toxic. They're both from the same family, but one is an evil twin.

All the leavy greens and herbs are shallow-rooted, meaning that special care needs to be taken when cultivating to manage weeds. Shallow roots also means that soil water availability is tensioned between gravity, evaporation, and cation exchange capacity (CEC). As we know, CEC is improved in the presence of organic matter, i.e., compost.

Evaporation can be managed by using mulch to cover the ground, which also acts as insulation and weed control. Watering should be more regular, totaling 1 inch (25 mm) per week. It's critical that soil gets kept moist up to 6 inches (15 cm) deep without it becoming waterlogged. Raised beds and ample organic material will help, and if you have the budget, including either perlite, pumice, chick grit, or biochar pellets is not a bad idea.

## Managing Apiaceae Root Vegetables

Carrots and parsnips have similar needs, and of the five main carrot varieties, parsnip is most like Danvers.

# PARSLEY FAMILY (*APIACEAE*)

| Five Main Carrot Varieties | | | | | |
|---|---|---|---|---|---|
| Type | Length in Inches (cm) | Top Diameter in Inches (cm) | Seed Spacing in Inches (cm) | Row Spacing in Inches (cm) | Days to Maturity |
| 'Chantenay' | 4–7 (10–18) | 2–2.5 (5–6) | 0.5, thin to 1 to 2 (1, thin to 2.5 to 5) | 12 (30) | 65–75 |
| 'Imperator' | 7–8 (18–20) | 1.5 (4) | 1, thin to 2 to 3 (2.5, thin to 5 to 8) | 18 (45) | 70 |
| 'Danvers' | 7 (18) | 2–2.5 (5–6) | 0.5, thin to 1 to 2 (1, thin to 2 to 5) | 12 (30) | 75 |
| 'Nantes' | 6–7 (15–18) | 1.5 (4) | 0.5, thin to 1 to 2 (1, thin to 2 to 5) | 12 (30) | 32–75 |
| 'Oxheart' | 2–3 (5–8) | 2 (5) | 3–5 (8–13) | 12 to 18 (30–45) | 90 |

## *Apiaceae Fertilizer Recommendations*

Recommended NPK fertilizers for this group are listed below. Recommendations are for soil of medium fertility in a 4 × 10–foot (1.2 × 3–m) bed and represent the total needs per season. Please do not exceed recommendations and subtract any nitrogen values that might be soilborne due to organic matter and legume cover crops. Start with less and respond to your plant's needs. Distributed feeding is better than occasional bulk feeding, unless you are boosting base in-soil fertility before planting, as informed by current valid soil-test results.

| Recommended NPK Fertilizers | | | | | | | | |
|---|---|---|---|---|---|---|---|---|
| Crop | N Starter | | N Side-dressing | | Phosphorus (P) | | Potassium (K) | |
| Carrots | 0.44 oz | 12.11 g | 0.44 oz | 12.11 g | 1.47 oz | 40.35 g | 1.47 oz | 40.35 g |
| Celery | 0.73 oz | 20.18 g | 0.59 oz | 16.14 g | 1.47 oz | 40.35 g | 1.47 oz | 40.35 g |
| Parsnip | 0.44 oz | 12.11 g | 0.44 oz | 12.11 g | 1.47 oz | 40.35 g | 1.47 oz | 40.35 g |

In case the numbers above seem small, the recommended starter application of nitrogen for carrots is 30 pounds per acre (start application). There are 43,560 square feet per acre and there is 16 ounces per pound. 30 pounds divided into 43,560 gives you 0.000689 pounds per square foot, or 0.0110193 ounces. A bed measuring 10 × 4 feet = 40 square feet will then need 0.440771 ounces of nitrogen.

The numbers are based on commercial farming recommendations and can help gardeners gain some insights in their application. Please note that the recommendations are for actual nitrogen, 10–10–10 mix only offers 10 percent nitrogen. A 0.44 ounce application will therefore need 4.4 ounces of fertilizer for a 40-square foot bed, or 121 grams for a 3.6-meter bed.[79]

A beautiful row of lavender plants just beginning to flower, growing alongside the polytunnel at Simplify Gardening, adds a touch of color and fragrance to the garden.

## Mitigating Non-Brassica Leafy Herbs and Vegetable Risks (Group 4)

Plants included in the non-brassica leafy vegetables and herbs group: arugula (rocket), basil, chicory, chive, cilantro (coriander), cress, dill, endive, escarole, fennel, Florence fennel, head lettuce, lavender, leaf lettuce, marjoram, oregano, parsley, radicchio, rosemary, sage, savory, spinach, Swiss chard, tarragon, thyme. Note that these risks extend to plants beyond the Apiaceae family to include some from the Asteraceae, Amaranthaceae, and Lamiaceae families.

### Common Pests

Aphids, caterpillars, flea beetles, leafhoppers, leaf miners, mites, slugs, and tarnished plant bug are all pests to look out for.

| Common Diseases and Their Related Pathogens | | |
|---|---|---|
| **Disease** | **Pathogen** | **Prevention** |
| Aster Yellows (Purple-top Wilt) | Phytoplasma mollicutes | • Remove infected plants.<br>• Manage leafhoppers.<br>• Ensure seed hygiene. |
| Bottom Rot (mainly lettuce) | *Rhizoctonia solani* fungus | • Water consistently.<br>• Manage soil temperatures: *Rhizoctonia solani* prefers 77°F to 81°F (25°C to 27°C). |
| Damping-off Seed and Seedling Rots | Various pathogens, including *Fusarium* spp. and *Pythium* spp. | • Ensure general hygiene.<br>• Use warmer water, 68°F to 77°F (20°C 25°C).<br>• Improve drainage. |
| Downy Mildew (mainly lettuce) | *Bremia* oomycete or *Peronospora* oomycete | • Improve soil drainage.<br>• Rotate crops.<br>• Avoid excessive humidity, leaf-wetting, and waterlogged soil. |

# PARSLEY FAMILY (*APIACEAE*)

| Common Diseases and Their Related Pathogens | | |
|---|---|---|
| **Disease** | **Pathogen** | **Prevention** |
| Gray Mold | *Botrytis* fungus | · Employ effective post-crop hygiene.<br>· Ensure adequate airflow (plant spacing).<br>· Remove infected plants. |
| Nematodes | Nematodes | · Increase soil compost content to boost beneficial microorganism populations.<br>· Consider anaerobic soil disinfection (ASD), a form of soil solarization.[80] |
| Powdery Mildew | *Golovinomyces cichoracearum* (formerly *Erysiphe cichoracearum* ) | · Rotate to non-host crops for three years.<br>· Ensure adequate airflow and drainage; use raised beds.<br>· Destroy finished crops to prevent disease buildup. |
| Lettuce Mosaic Virus (LMV) (also affects escarole, endive, pea, and spinach) | Various pathogens | · Ensure seed hygiene.<br>· Manage aphids.<br>· Manage weeds. |
| White Mold (Timber Rot, Drop, Stem Rot) | *Sclerotinia* fungus | · Destroy (burn) infected crops and weeds.<br>· Manage weeds. |
| White Rust (mainly spinach and mustard) | Mainly *Albugo candida*, but there are thousands of rust-causing fungi (oomycete) species | · Ensure seed hygiene: 122°F (50°C) for 25 minutes.<br>· Use crop rotation.<br>· Ensure adequate airflow and drainage; use raised beds. |
| Fusarium wilt | *Fusarium oxysporum* f. sp. *lycopersici* | · Ensure general hygiene.<br>· Ensure seed hygiene.<br>· Destroy infected crops (burn).<br>· Use crop rotation.<br>· Avoid excessive nitrogen.<br>· Manage soil acidity. |

# COMPOSITE FAMILY (*ASTERACEAE*)

| Common Name | Botanical Name | Management Approach (EPA) |
|---|---|---|
| Artichokes | *Cynara cardunculus* var. *scolymus* | Group 1: Root and Tuber Vegetables |
| Endives | *Cichorium endivia, C. intybus* (Belgian endive) | Group 4: Leafy Greens and Leafy Petioles |
| Lettuce | *Lactuca sativa* | Group 4: Leafy Greens and Leafy Petioles |
| Sunflowers | *Helianthus annuus* | Group 20: Oilseeds |

## Managing Asteraceae Crops

The family consists of cool-season annuals (excluding the perennial artichoke). Included is the sunflower, but it is worth knowing that sunflower hosts weevils, so depending on the crops you're growing, you may want to limit its proximity. We covered the leafy green pests and diseases in the previous section and noticed the need for raised beds that drain well and avoiding planting crops too close to each other, ensuring optimal airflow.

### *Lettuce*

When lettuce is exposed to high temperatures, prolonged daylight, high humidity, or dry soil, it will bolt, causing deteriorated quality (bitterness). Looseleaf lettuce, one of four popular types, can be harvested forty to fifty days after planting. The loosely formed head of a butterhead, also known as a Boston or Bibb, is the second most popular variety. Cos, sometimes known as romaine, stands tall and narrow and does well even in higher temperatures.

[top] A magnificent sunflower with vibrant yellow petals is in full bloom, standing tall and brightening up the garden with its cheerful presence.

[bottom] Here I am picking outer leaves from a lettuce bed at Simplify Gardening. Expert harvesting means continuous growth and sustainability.

Cos and butterhead grow to maturity in sixty to seventy days. Iceberg or crisphead is the most challenging to cultivate due to its great sensitivity to heat and lengthy maturation period of seventy to one hundred twenty days.

Seeds should be planted outside four weeks before the typical last frost date. It also is possible to use transplants that were started indoors about three weeks before the outdoor planting season. Soil temperature (at a 4-inch (10 cm) depth) needs to be at least 40°F (4.4°C). Set your lettuce seeds 6 to 8 inches (15 to 20 cm) apart if you're growing butterhead or cos, but only 2 to 4 inches (5 to 10 cm) if you're growing looseleaf. Lettuce and endive require a minimum of 8 inches (20 cm) between rows. Plant leaf lettuce 4 to 6 inches (10 to 15 cm) apart in a wide row. Lettuce is tolerant of partial shade, particularly when temperatures rise.

Stagger planting every two weeks while the weather stays cool to ensure a steady lettuce supply (the last planting should be four weeks before the hot weather of summer begins). A 10-foot (3-m) row can produce 5 pounds (2.2 kg) of leaf lettuce or fifteen to twenty-four heads of butterhead or cos lettuce. You should get back to planting in late summer, around August. If the temperature forecasts indicate a drop into the high 20s°F (below the freezing point), cover lettuce rows with row covers.

### *Endive*

Harvesting time for endive and escarole is around eighty to one hundred days. Endive and escarole, which are both heat-sensitive and require a long time to mature, are exclusively cultivated as a spring crop, where they are planted about four weeks before the typical last frost date. Either sow seeds direct into the garden or start transplants indoors to give yourself a head start. Plant in rows no closer than 18 inches (46 cm) apart, and at a maximum spacing of 9 to 12 inches (23 to 30 cm) between plants. Planting season begins four weeks before the average last frost date and continues for one week beyond. It's best to sow a fall crop in July. As a rule, the last planting date should be done around two months before the typical first frost date.

Ensure the plants are consistently hydrated, especially in warmer weather. Both endive and escarole are quite resilient, making them perfect for harvesting all through

Numerous pots filled with delicate lettuce seedlings are each eagerly awaiting transplanting into the garden where they can continue to grow and thrive.

In this lush bed of lettuce, a vibrant endive plant stands out, adding diversity and a unique texture to the verdant garden scene.

the fall. If development stalls, use a small amount of a high-nitrogen fertilizer as a side-dressing. Blanching plants prior to harvest reduces their bitterness and turns them a pale yellow or white. Cover the plants for a week or two, or tie the large outer leaves up over the head like you would with cauliflower. It's important to dry the head thoroughly before blanching to avoid rotting. Heads are ready to harvest between eighty and one hundred days after planting. Remove all leaves, including the tough outer ones and the roots, by cutting the plant off at the soil line. If the temperature rises significantly after planting in the spring, you should get the harvest over with. If a severe freeze is predicted for fall, harvest. Yield per 10-foot (3-m) row should be about 6 pounds (2.7 kg).

### Asteraceae Fertilizer Recommendations

Recommended NPK fertilizers for this group are listed below. Recommendations are for soil of medium fertility in a 4 × 10–foot bed (given in ounces) or a 1.2 × 3–meter bed (given in grams) and represent to total needs per season. Please do not exceed recommendations and subtract any nitrogen values that might be soilborne due to organic matter and legume cover crops. Start with less and respond to your plant's needs. Distributed feeding is better than occasional bulk feeding, unless you are boosting base in-soil fertility before planting, as informed by current valid soil-test results.

## COMPOSITE FAMILY (*ASTERACEAE*)

| Recommended NPK Fertilizers | | | | | | | | |
|---|---|---|---|---|---|---|---|---|
| Crop | N Starter | | N Side-dressing | | Phosphorus (P) | | Potassium (K) | |
| Lettuce, Endive, and Escarole | 0.88 oz | 24.21 g | 0.44 oz | 12.11 g | 2.20 oz | 60.53 g | 2.20 oz | 60.53 g |

# MUSTARD FAMILY (*BRASSICACEAE*)

| Common Name | Botanical Name | Management Approach (EPA) |
|---|---|---|
| Broccoli | *Brassica oleracea* var. *italica* | Group 5: Cole Crops and Brassica Leafy Greens |
| Brussels Sprouts | *Brassica oleracea* var. *gemmifera* | Group 5: Cole Crops and Brassica Leafy Greens |
| Cabbage | *Brassica oleracea* var. *capitata* | Group 5: Cole Crops and Brassica Leafy Greens |
| Cauliflower | *Brassica oleracea* var. *botrytis* | Group 5: Cole Crops and Brassica Leafy Greens |
| Kale | *Brassica oleracea* var. *acephala* | Group 5: Cole Crops and Brassica Leafy Greens |
| Kohlrabi | *Brassica oleracea* var. *gongylodes* | Group 5: Cole Crops and Brassica Leafy Greens |
| Mustard | *Brassica juncea* | Group 5: Cole Crops and Brassica Leafy Greens |
| Radishes | *Raphanus sativus* | Group 1: Root and Tuber Vegetables |
| Rutabaga | *Brassica napus* | Group 1: Root and Tuber Vegetables |
| Turnip | *Brassica rapa* | Group 1: Root and Tuber Vegetables |

## Managing Cole Crops and Brassica Leafy Greens

Brassica plants belong to EPA's Group 5 crops (Cole Crops and Brassica Leafy Greens). Notice the distinction as it implies there are two management approaches to the Brassicaceae family. The cole crops include broccoli, Brussels sprouts, cabbage, cauliflower, and kohlrabi, and the brassica leafy greens include collards, kale, and mustard. Brassica root crops include turnip (*Brassica rapa*) and rutabaga (*Brassica napus*).

A healthy swede/rutabaga plant thriving directly in the soil. Its strong green leaves spreading wide as its root develops beneath the ground.

An impressive display of purple and white Milan turnips growing in the garden, with their vibrant colors and healthy foliage. These turnips demonstrate the benefits of minimal maintenance, requiring only two side-dressing per year to flourish.

## Cole Crops and Brassica Leafy Greens Fertilizer Recommendations

Recommended NPK fertilizers for this group are listed below. Recommendations are for soil of medium fertility in a 4 × 10–foot bed (given in ounces) or a 1.2 × 3–meter bed (given in grams). Please do not exceed recommendations and subtract any nitrogen values that might be soilborne due to organic matter and legume cover crops. Start with less and respond to your plant's needs.

Distributed feeding is better than occasional bulk feeding, unless you are boosting base in-soil fertility before planting, as informed by current valid soil-test results. Phosphorus and potassium quantities as well and the nitrogen starter are added to the soil before planting. The side-dressing quantity reflected in the table below is for the first application quantity that should be added two to three weeks after planting. A second side-dressing can be repeated three weeks later, depending on the weather (fertilizer is immobilized in cold weather) and the plant's progress. The second side-dressing application **should not be more than half of the first (listed) side-dressing quantity.**

The brassica root crops (rutabaga and turnips) **should not get a second nitrogen side-dressing, but will benefit from some boron.**

### *Boron*

Radish, rutabaga, and turnips will benefit with an application of boron—0.02 ounces per 40-square foot bed or 0.61 grams per 3.6-square meter bed. Make a batch that includes a bulking agent to help get a lower concentration for easier spreading. Generally, boron applications are a pound or two per acre and the above calculations are based on 1.5 pounds (680 g) per acre. Most vegetable crops benefit from a boron application (same ratio), excluding the Fabaceae, Cucurbitaceae, and Asteraceae families. Also don't add it to herb and spinach crops.

| Recommended NPK Fertilizers | | | | | | | | |
|---|---|---|---|---|---|---|---|---|
| **Crop** | **N Starter** | | **N Side-dressings** | | **Phosphorus (P)** | | **Potassium (K)** | |
| Broccoli | 1.10 oz | 30.26 g | 0.73 oz | 20.18 g | 1.47 oz | 40.35 g | 1.47 oz | 40.35 g |
| Brussels Sprouts, Cabbage, and Cauliflower | 0.88 oz | 24.21 g | 0.59 oz | 16.14 g | 1.47 oz | 40.35 g | 1.47 oz | 40.35 g |
| Collard, Kale, and Mustard | 0.73 oz | 20.18 g | 0.44 oz | 12.11 g | 1.47 oz | 40.35 g | 1.47 oz | 40.35 g |
| Radishes*, Rutabaga, and Turnips | 0.54 oz | 14.93 g | 0.44 oz | 12.11 g | 1.47 oz | 40.35 g | 1.47 oz | 40.35 g |

* Radishes do not require a side-dressing application as their emergence and time-to-maturity doesn't justify it.

## Mitigating Cole Crops and Brassica Leafy Greens Risks (Group 5)

### *Common Pests*

- Cabbage aphids, flea beetles, leaf miners, seed and root maggots, stink bugs, swede midge, and thrips.

- Root maggots: White maggots (larvae) attack all plants of the cabbage family. Larvae tunnel in and feed on roots of plants. Early maggot damage includes plant wilting, eventually causing the plants to die.

- Yellow-margined leaf-beetle (YMLB), especially on turnips and Napa cabbage. Turnip trap crops and insecticide applications can reduce population buildups. Insect netting or row covers can block migratory adults.

- Snails and Slugs: Populations increase in areas with frequent rainfall and soil with high organic matter content. Do not over-irrigate and remove crop debris to reduce slug and snail population buildups.

- Caterpillars including cabbage looper, cabbageworm, cabbage webworm, and armyworms.

Here you see a magnified leaf infested with thrips, which are tiny insects that can cause damage to plants. Their presence on the leaf highlights the importance of regular monitoring and integrated pest management to maintain the health and productivity of the garden.

Prevention measures include rotating away from brassica crops for at least three years. Swede midge can be hosted by brassica weeds such as yellow rocket, shepherd's purse, and wild mustard, so weed management is essential. Smash crops and incorporate crop residue up to 8 inches (20 cm) into the soil soon after harvesting—it acts as a soil fumigant. Brassica seed meals are used for the same purpose (especially mustard seeds).

| Common Diseases | | |
|---|---|---|
| **Disease** | **Pathogen** | **Prevention** |
| Black Leg | *Phoma lingam* fungus | • Ensure seed hygiene.<br>• Use four-year brassica plants rotation.<br>• Rogue diseased plants.<br>• Ensure good soil drainage and air circulation.<br>• Manage brassica weeds.<br>• Avoid working in the fields when wet.<br>• Cauliflower, broccoli, and turnip cultivars are moderately susceptible.<br>• Rutabaga, radish, and mustard cultivars are less susceptible. |
| Black Rot | *Xanthomonas campestris* pv. *campestris* bacteria | • Ensure seed hygiene.<br>• Ensure general hygiene.<br>• Use four-year brassica plants rotation.<br>• Manage weeds.<br>• Rogue diseased plants (burn them).<br>• Ensure good soil drainage and air circulation.<br>• Avoid overhead irrigation. |

## Common Diseases

| Disease | Pathogen | Prevention |
|---|---|---|
| Bottom Rot | *Rhizoctonia solani* fungus | • Practice watering consistency.<br>• Manage soil temperatures: *Rhizoctonia solani* prefers 77°F to 81°F (25°C to 27°C). |
| Club Root | *Plasmodiophora* fungus | • Tough to manage once established.<br>• Buy resistant cultivars.<br>• Ensure seed hygiene.<br>• Maintain a pH of above 7.1 using calcitic lime and adjusted boron will be required.<br>• Improve soil drainage.<br>• Practice brassica weed management. |
| Damping-off Seed and Seedling Rots | Various pathogens, including *Fusarium* spp. and *Pythium* spp. | • Ensure general hygiene.<br>• Use warmer water, 68°F to 77°F (20°C to 25°C).<br>• Improve drainage. |
| Downy Mildew | *Hyaloperonospora* oomycete | • Improve soil drainage.<br>• Rotate crops.<br>• Avoid excessive humidity, leaf-wetting, and waterlogged soil. |
| Leaf Spot | *Alternaria, Ascochyta, Cercospora,* and *Septoria* fungi | • Buy certified, disease-free seed, or disease-resistant cultivars.<br>• Ensure seed hygiene.<br>• Ensure general hygiene.<br>• Use four-year brassica plants rotation.<br>• Practice brassica weed management.<br>• Incorporate diseased plant debris into the soil immediately after harvest.<br>• Ensure good drainage, airflow, and minimize overhead watering.<br>• Control flea beetles. |
| Powdery Mildew | *Golovinomyces cichoracearum* fungus | • Ensure seed hygiene.<br>• Ensure general hygiene.<br>• Use four-year brassica plants rotation.<br>• Practice brassica weed management.<br>• Ensure adequate airflow—low humidity buildup.<br>• Water inhibits spore germination for most powdery mildews. Only jet-spray leaves if other leaf diseases are not a problem. |
| White Mold (Timber Rot, Drop, Stem Rot) | *Sclerotinia* fungus | • Destroy (burn) infected crops and weeds.<br>• Manage weeds. |
| White Rust | *Albugo* oomycete | • Ensure seed hygiene: 122°F (50°C) for 25 minutes.<br>• Use crop rotation.<br>• Ensure adequate airflow and drainage; use raised beds. |
| Wirestem | *Rhizoctonia solani* fungus | • Use well-draining raised beds.<br>• Use rye as a rotation crop, as it isn't susceptible to wirestem causing *Rhizoctonia solani.*<br>• Avoid planting legume cover crops immediately before cole crops. |
| Yellows | *Fusarium oxysporum* f. sp. *lycopersici* | • Ensure general hygiene.<br>• Ensure seed hygiene.<br>• Destroy infected crops (burn).<br>• Use crop rotation.<br>• Avoid excessive nitrogen.<br>• Manage soil acidity. |

# BINDWEED FAMILY (*CONVOLVULACEAE*)

The only member of the bindweed family we're interested in is the sweet potato. The morning glory also belongs to the Convolvulaceae family and the purple sweet potato vine often is used, not as a food, but as a popular ornamental plant.

### *Sweet Potato (Ipomoea batatas)*

Whereas potatoes are tuberous stems, the sweet potato is an actual root from a vining plant from the morning-glory family. Management strategies to be followed are for EPA Group 1: Root and Tuber Vegetables. Although they come in a rainbow of colors, the edible tuberous roots often have a burgundy skin and an orange flesh. They are ample suppliers of beta-carotene, vitamins $B_6$ and C, potassium, and fiber. Anthocyanin content is higher in purple sweet potatoes. They can be consumed both raw and cooked.

Here you see sweet potatoes nestled in a compost seed tray, sprouting vibrant green slips. These slips indicate the beginning of their growth journey, promising an abundance of tasty and nutritious tubers. The carefully prepared compost seed tray ensures the slips have the ideal environment to flourish.

| | | | |
|---|---|---|---|
| **Also Called:** | Sweet potato | **Root Health:** | Prefer soil with high organic content that drains well |
| **Difficulty:** | Easy | **Soil Temperature:** | Ideal 77°F (25°C) |
| **Ambient Temperature:** | Warm season (hot) | **Soil pH:** | 6.0 to 6.8 |
| **Hardiness Zones:** | 9 to 11 | **Tolerance:** | Will tolerate occasionally dry soil |
| **Life Cycle:** | Perennial | **Emergence:** | 7 days |
| **Light:** | Full sun to partial shade | **Airflow:** | Need ample space |
| **Height:** | 6 to 10 feet (1.8 to 3 m) | **Spread:** | 8 to 10 feet (2.4 to 3 m) |
| **Notes:** | Plant sweet potato slips outdoors three to four weeks after your last spring frost or once the soil at a depth of 4 inches (10 cm) has warmed to at least 65°F (18°C). | | |

# CUCURBIT FAMILY (*CUCURBITACEAE*)

| Common Name | Botanical Name | Management Approach (EPA) |
|---|---|---|
| Cucumbers | *Cucumis sativus* | Group 9: Cucurbit Vegetables |
| Melons | *Benincasa hispida* | Group 9: Cucurbit Vegetables |
| Squashes (Summer) | *Cucurbita pepo* | Group 9: Cucurbit Vegetables |
| Squashes (Winter) | *Cucurbita maxima, C. pepo, C. moschata* | Group 9: Cucurbit Vegetables |
| Pumpkins | *Cucurbita maxima* | Group 9: Cucurbit Vegetables |
| Gourds | *Lagenaria siceraria* | Group 9: Cucurbit Vegetables |

## Managing Cucurbit Vegetables

Cucurbit plants are easy to grow and produce abundant fruits in warm weather. To grow cucurbit plants, you need to follow these steps:

1. Choose a sunny location with well-drained soil and plenty of space for the vines to spread.
2. Prepare the soil by adding compost or organic matter and loosening it with a fork or tiller.
3. Sow the seeds directly in the ground after the last frost date, or start them indoors three to four weeks earlier and transplant them when the soil is warm.
4. Plant the seeds about 1-inch (2.5-cm) deep and 2 to 3 feet (61 to 91 cm) apart in rows or hills. Water them well and keep the soil moist but not soggy.
5. Thin the seedlings, leaving one or two vigorous plants per hill or row.
6. Pinch off any flowers that appear before the plants have five to six leaves to encourage more growth.
7. Fertilize the plants every two to three weeks with a balanced fertilizer or compost tea. Avoid high-nitrogen fertilizers that can cause excessive foliage and poor fruiting.

I've grown an impressively large cucumber in my polytunnel. The cucumber's size and healthy appearance are a testament to my gardening expertise and the nurturing conditions provided by the polytunnel.

(continued on page 150)

This is my impressive cucumber entry at the Malvern Autumn Show, showcasing the fruits of my labor and dedication to cultivating exceptional produce in the competitive horticultural arena.

This awe-inspiring image of a thriving Giant Marrow patch at Simplify Gardening's garden, reveals the dedication and skill involved in nurturing these extraordinary vegetables to reach their remarkable size and prominence.

A delicate female pumpkin flower in full bloom. Look at the intricate details, ovary bulge below the flower, vibrant colors, and natural beauty that play a crucial role in the development of this beloved autumn vegetable.

A male pumpkin flower displays its vivid colors and intricate details, highlighting the importance of this often-overlooked component in the pollination process for successful pumpkin growth.

8.  Mulch the plants with straw or grass clippings to conserve moisture and suppress weeds. You can use trellises or cages to support the vines and keep the fruits off the ground.
9.  Monitor the plants for pests and diseases and treat them accordingly. Common problems include aphids, squash bugs, cucumber beetles, powdery mildew, and mosaic virus.
10. Harvest the fruits when they are ripe and enjoy them fresh or preserved. Cucurbit plants can produce for several weeks until the first frost kills them.

The cucurbits have a special flowering habit that requires insect pollination for fruit sets. The cucurbits produce separate male and female flowers on the same plant (monoecious). The male flowers usually appear before the female flowers. The female flowers are open for only one day and need to receive enough pollen from the male flowers to develop into full-size fruits. The appearance of female and pollinating flowers in cucurbits depends on several factors, such as temperature, planting density, nitrogen fertilization, and day length.

Generally, higher temperatures and longer days promote more female flowers, while lower temperatures and shorter days favor more male flowers. However, extreme temperatures can reduce flower production and pollination efficiency.

Planting density and nitrogen fertilization can affect the balance between vegetative and reproductive growth and thus influence the number and quality of flowers. To ensure good pollination and fruit set in cucurbits, it is crucial to provide optimal growing conditions, attract and protect pollinators, and monitor the flowering patterns of the plants.

[top right] A female squash flower, secured with a tie to prevent cross-pollination. The remnants of two male flowers used for pollination can be seen nearby, illustrating the gardener's careful and deliberate efforts to control the plant's genetic outcome.

[bottom right] A thriving pumpkin seedling with an impressive white root system is captured in this photo, signifying its readiness to be transplanted into the garden and begin its journey toward becoming a fully grown, healthy pumpkin.

## Fertilizer Recommendations for Cucurbit Vegetables

Do not exceed recommendations and subtract any nitrogen values that might be soilborne due to organic matter and legume cover crops. Start with less and respond to your plant's needs. Distributed feeding is better than occasional bulk feeding, unless you are boosting base in-soil fertility before planting, as informed by current valid soil-test results. Phosphorus and potassium quantities as well and the nitrogen starter are added to the soil before planting. In the table below the imperial amounts are for a 40-square foot bed (10 × 4 ft) and the metric amounts are for a 3.6-meter bed (3 × 1.2 m). Cucurbits are notoriously hungry for potash (K), so boost their supply, but exclude summer squash varieties. It's an ideal solution to incorporate the nitrogen side-dressing amount into your irrigation system, spreading the feed (side-dressing quantity) as the vines run. Incorporate some P and K into your side-dressing, about a quarter of the total initial amount.

Here you see a young, immature cucumber still growing on the vine. The tiny fruit is beginning to develop its characteristic shape and color, showcasing the early stages of growth in the life cycle of a cucumber plant.

| Recommended NPK Fertilizers | | | | | | | | |
|---|---|---|---|---|---|---|---|---|
| Crop | N Starter | | N Side-dressings | | Phosphorus (P) | | Potassium (K) | |
| Cucumber | 1.03 oz | 28.25 g | 0.37 oz | 10.09 g | 1.47 oz | 40.35 g | 2.20 oz | 60.53 g |
| Melons (Cantaloupes) | 0.59 oz | 16.14 g | 0.37 oz | 10.09 g | 1.47 oz | 40.35 g | 2.20 oz | 60.53 g |
| Pumpkin | 1.18 oz | 32.28 g | 0.59 oz | 16.14 g | 1.47 oz | 40.35 g | 2.20 oz | 60.53 g |
| Winter Squash | 1.18 oz | 32.28 g | 0.59 oz | 16.14 g | 1.47 oz | 40.35 g | 2.20 oz | 60.53 g |
| Summer Squash | 0.73 oz | 20.18 g | 0.44 oz | 12.11 g | 1.47 oz | 40.35 g | 1.47 oz | 40.35 g |
| Watermelon | 0.73 oz | 20.18 g | 0.44 oz | 12.11 g | 1.47 oz | 40.35 g | 2.20 oz | 60.53 g |

## Mitigating Cucurbit Vegetable Risks (Group 9)

Because pathogens can quickly adapt to resistance genes and chemical modes of action, controlling disease in cucurbits demands vigilance.

### Common Pests

Aphids, cucumber beetles, leafhoppers, mites, seed and root maggots, slugs, squash bugs, squash vine borer, thrips, whiteflies, and wireworms are common to cucurbit crops.

A determined slug is seen making its way across a patch of dry dirt, highlighting the resilience and adaptability of these garden pests as they navigate their environment in search of food or shelter.

| Common Diseases | | |
|---|---|---|
| **Disease** | **Pathogen** | **Prevention** |
| Angular Leaf Spot | *Pseudomonas* bacteria | • Buy clean seed from a reputable source.<br>• Ensure seed hygiene.<br>• Use crop rotation to non-cucurbit families.<br>• Use drip irrigation instead of overhead sprinklers.<br>• Do not work in plants when leaves are wet.<br>• Rouge infected fruit and vines at the end of the season. |
| Anthracnose | *Colletotrichum* fungus | • Purchase disease-free seed.<br>• Ensure seed hygiene.<br>• Use crop rotation to non-cucurbit families.<br>• Avoid working beds when the foliage is wet.<br>• If practical, avoid wetting foliage, else water early in the day, allowing foliage to dry fast.<br>• Source resistant watermelon and cucumber cultivars.<br>• Anthracnose is more severe in late summer. |
| Bacterial Fruit Blotch | *Acidovorax* bacteria | • Use clean seed and disease-free transplants.<br>• Practice hygiene management.<br>• Ensure good airflow and drainage.<br>• Avoid sprinkler irrigation and working in beds when the foliage is wet. |
| Bacterial Wilt | *Erwinia tracheiphila,*<br>*Ralstonia solanacearum* bacteria | • Employ cucumber beetle control.<br>• Use row covers to suppress bacterial wilt transmission.<br>• Use crop rotation to reduce beetle numbers in adjacent areas.<br>• Rogue infected plants.<br>• Spunbonded row covers will exclude beetles.<br>• Plant a trap crop of Blue Hubbard squash to protect more susceptible crops. |

## Common Diseases

| Disease | Pathogen | Prevention |
|---|---|---|
| Damping-off Seed and Seedling Rots | Various pathogens, including *Fusarium* spp. and *Pythium* spp. | • Ensure general hygiene.<br>• Use warmer water, 68°F to 77°F (20°C to 25°C) when watering.<br>• Improve drainage. |
| Downy Mildew | *Pseudoperonospora* oomycete | • Partially resistant varieties of cucumber and cantaloupe are available.<br>• Avoid planting cucumbers late that will only yield after early July—the high-risk hot season.<br>• Avoid wet foliage.<br>• Rouge infected plants. |
| Fruit Rot | *Fusarium* fungus | • Ensure good airflow and fast draining soil; use raised beds.<br>• Prevent foliage from getting (or staying) wet.<br>• Manage foliage disease.<br>• Use crop rotation.<br>• Start with disease-free seed or use fungicide-treated seeds. |
| Fusarium Wilt | *Fusarium* fungus | • Ensure a soil pH 6.0–7.0.<br>• Reduce nitrogen levels.<br>• Use resistant varieties, such as the Athena cantaloupe. |
| Gummy Stem Blight/Black Rot (Mainly in the Cucurbit family) | *Didymella* bryoniae or *Phoma cucurbitacearum* fungus | • Use pathogen-free seed.<br>• Crop-rotate to non-cucurbit crops.<br>• Rouge finished crops to prevent disease buildup. |
| Leaf Blight | *Alternaria* or *Plectosporium* fungi | • Use disease-free seed.<br>• Ensure seed hygiene.<br>• Use crop rotation.<br>• Promptly rogue finished crops to prevent disease buildup.<br>• *Alternaria* is hosted by Solanaceae plants too, so don't plant cucurbits after tomatoes, peppers or eggplants, and vice versa. |
| Leaf Spot and Fruit Spot | *Xanthomonas* bacteria | • Ensure seed hygiene.<br>• Rotate to non-cucurbit family crops.<br>• Rouge finished crops as soon as possible. |
| Nematodes | Several nematode species | • Proliferation of beneficial microorganisms by compost additions.<br>• Anaerobic soil disinfestation (ASD) is an effective soil sterilization method.<br>• Promptly rogue finished crops to prevent disease buildup. |
| Phytophthora Blight | *Phytophthora* oomycete | • Use disease-free seed.<br>• Ensure seed hygiene.<br>• Use crop rotation.<br>• Promptly rogue finished crops to prevent disease buildup. |
| Powdery Mildew | *Podosphaera* fungus | • Similar response to Phytophthora blight. |
| Scabs | *Cladosporium* fungus | • Similar response as for powdery mildew. |
| Viruses | Several species | • Manage aphid populations as they spread viruses.<br>• Ensure seed health.<br>• Ensure seed hygiene. |

# YAM FAMILY (*DIOSCOREACEAE*)

The Yam family is not a staple of home vegetable gardens, but there are several types of yams worth growing.

### Yams: *Dioscorea* Vegetables

To grow yams, you need a warm and humid climate, well-drained soil, and a trellis or stake to support the vines. Start yams from seeds, cuttings, or small tubers. Plant them in early spring, about 6 inches (15 cm) deep and 3 feet (91 cm) apart. Water them regularly and fertilize them every two weeks with a balanced fertilizer. Harvest them when the leaves start to yellow and die back, usually after six to ten months. Store them in a cool and dry place away from sunlight.

Some of the most common types of yams in the United States are:

**American yam:** This is actually a type of sweet potato with red skin and orange flesh. It is soft and moist when cooked, and often used for holiday dishes such as candied yams or sweet potato pie.

**Japanese mountain yam:** This is a cylindrical yam with light brown skin and white flesh. When grated or cut, it has a slimy texture and often is eaten raw in salads or sushi.

**Tropical yam:** This broad category includes many species of yams that grow in tropical regions. They have thick skins and starchy flesh that can be white, yellow, purple, or pink. They are usually boiled, roasted, or fried, and can be made into soups, stews, or fritters.

**Filipino purple yam:** Also known as ube or ubi, this yam has a deep purple color that makes it famous for desserts. It has a sweet and nutty flavor and can be mashed, baked, or turned into ice cream, cake, or pudding.

# CASSAVA FAMILY (*EUPHORBIACEAE*)

*Manihot esculenta*, the epithet means good to eat, is loaded with cyanogens, requiring several processes such as boiling or fermenting before it can safely be consumed. The whole process reminds me of cacao, *Theobroma* (food of the gods). Fresh cacao beans are loaded with cyanogens, and only after the natural fermentation process are they fit for human consumption. I often wonder about the Aztec tasters and the discovery process for using these naturally toxic foods. Cassava is vegetatively propagated from healthy stem cuttings from plants not older than a year. Plants should be spaced 39 inches (1 m) apart in rows similarly spaced. The plant does better if intercropped with the Fabaceae family (beans, peas), as these legume crops fix nitrogen for higher harvests. Soil temperature must be above 77°F (25°C), and the soil moist for initial growth. Planting generally commences at the start of the rainy season but often is linked to intercropping needs.

Cassava is not a common garden plant, but with the right know-how you can grow it at home.

| | | | |
|---|---|---|---|
| **Also Called:** | Yuka, Manioc | **Root Health:** | Consistently moist, fertile, sandy, well-drained soils |
| **Difficulty:** | Medium | **Soil Temperature:** | 77°F (25°C) |
| **Ambient Temperature:** | Tropics | **Soil pH:** | 6.0 to 7.0 |
| **Hardiness Zones:** | 10 to 12 | **Tolerance:** | Intolerant of frost but will re-emerge |
| **Life Cycle:** | Woody shrub, evergreen | **Emergence:** | Needs 8 to 9 months frost-free growth season |
| **Light:** | Full sun to partial shade | **Airflow:** | Space well apart |
| **Height:** | 6 to 10 feet (1.8 to 3 m) | **Spread:** | 6 to 10 feet (1.8 to 3 m) |
| **Notes:** | Unprocessed roots and leaves are toxic (Cyanogenic glycosides linamarin and lotaustralin). | | |

# PEA FAMILY (FABACEAE)

| Common Name | Botanical Name | Management Approach (EPA) |
|---|---|---|
| Beans | *Phaseolus vulgaris, P. coccineus* | Group 6: Legume Vegetables |
| Chickpeas | *Cicer arietinum* | Group 6: Legume Vegetables |
| Fava Beans | *Vicia faba* | Group 6: Legume Vegetables |
| Lentils | *Lens culinaris* | Group 6: Legume Vegetables |
| Lima Beans | *Phaseolus lunatus* | Group 6: Legume Vegetables |
| Peas | *Lathyrus oleraceus, Pisum sativum* | Group 6: Legume Vegetables |
| Soybeans | *Glycine max* | Group 6: Legume Vegetables |

## Managing Legume Vegetables

### *Beans*

Plant bush varieties of fresh or snap beans, dry beans, lima beans, and southern peas at a density of five to seven seeds per 1 foot (30 cm) of row for lima beans, sowing two to three seeds per 1 foot (30 cm) of row for southern peas. White mold is suppressed by increasing the distance between rows. After the soil has warmed to an average of 60°F (16°C) and the threat of frost has passed, you can plant these cool-season veggies. Bush snap beans can be planted in succession. Vining plants can be trained to climb an 8-foot (2.4-m)-tall trellis made of horticultural netting with no effort.

### *Peas*

Plant bush varieties at six to eight seeds per 1 foot (30 cm) of row and vining varieties at three to four seeds per 1 foot (30 cm) of row. These cool-season vegetables need to be sown in the early spring for a spring yield, or in the mid to late summer for a fall crop. In the summer's high temperatures, plants decline rapidly. Vines can be trained to climb a trellis made of horticultural netting up to 5 feet (1.5 m) in height.

Here, I'm in the process of transferring pea seedlings grown in a gutter into a garden trench. This innovative technique allows for easy transplantation and continued growth, ensuring a successful pea harvest in the future.

## Fertilizer Recommendations for Legume Vegetables

Do not exceed recommendations and subtract any nitrogen values that might be soilborne due to organic matter content. Start with less and respond to your plant's needs. Distributed feeding is better than occasional bulk feeding, unless you are boosting base in-soil fertility before planting, as informed by current valid soil-test results.

When the pH of the soil is above 6.5, zinc and manganese deficiencies might develop in beans. Banded fertilizer at planting time should contain up to 1 pound of zinc per acre (0.01 ounces per bed or 0.4 grams) and 2 pounds of manganese per acre (0.03 ounces per bed, or 0.8 grams). Up to 10 pounds of zinc per acre (0.15 ounces per bed, or 4 grams) can be broadcast if banding is not an option. If necessary, use foliar sprays.

Legumes should not be given additional nitrogen as they grow. Phosphorus and potassium quantities for peas are much lower than other plants but should be added to the soil before planting. In the table below the imperial amounts are for a 40-square foot bed (10 × 4 ft) and the metric amounts are for a 3.6-meter bed (3 × 1.2 m).

The remarkable size of this large bean pod was achieved with great care.

## Recommended NPK Fertilizers

| Crop | N Starter | | N Side-dressings | | Phosphorus (P) | | Potassium (K) | |
|---|---|---|---|---|---|---|---|---|
| Lima Bean | 0.54 oz | 14.93 g | 0 oz | 0 g | 0.88 oz | 24.21 g | 0.88 oz | 24.21 g |
| Snap Bean | 0.44 oz | 12.11 g | 0 oz | 0 g | 0.88 oz | 24.21 g | 0.88 oz | 24.21 g |
| English Pea | 0.73 oz | 20.18 g | 0 oz | 0 g | 1.18 oz | 32.28 g | 1.18 oz | 32.28 g |
| Southern Pea | 0.73 oz | 20.18 g | 0 oz | 0 g | 0.71 oz | 19.37 g | 0.71 oz | 19.37 g |

## Mitigating Legume Vegetable Risks (Group 6)

Because pathogens can quickly adapt to resistance genes and chemical modes of action, disease control in legume crops demands vigilance.

### *Common Pests*

Aphids, cucumber bean leaf beetles, caterpillars, cowpea curculio beetles, leafhoppers, Mexican bean beetles, mites, pea weevil beetles, seed and root maggots, stink bugs, thrips, and wireworms are common to different legume crops.

Peas are a popular member of the Fabaceae family. They are cool-season vegetables that prefer to grow in early spring or fall, when temperatures are lower.

## Common Diseases

| Disease | Pathogen | Prevention |
|---------|----------|------------|
| Anthracnose | *Colletotrichum* fungus | · Buy clean seed from a reputable source.<br>· Seek resistant cultivars.<br>· Use crop rotation with non-host families (corn).<br>· Rouge infected fruit and vines at the end of the season, adding to your compost bin (if you use traditional high temperature composting method described earlier). |
| Common Bacterial Blight | *Xanthomonas* bacteria | · Use disease-free seed.<br>· Ensure seed hygiene.<br>· Use crop rotation.<br>· Promptly rogue finished crops to prevent disease buildup. |
| Damping-off Seed and Seedling Rots | Various pathogens, including *Fusarium* spp. and *Pythium* spp. | · Ensure general hygiene.<br>· Use warmer water, 68°F to 77°F (20°C to 25°C).<br>· Improve drainage. |
| Gray Mold | *Botrytis* fungus | · Any beds with a gray mold history should NOT be used for broadleaf crops, dicots. Plant grass grains or sweet corn instead for at least six years.<br>· Rogue promptly to eliminate the host totally (burn). |
| Halo Blight | *Pseudomonas* bacteria | · Plant certified disease-free seed produced in arid regions unfavorable for development of bacterial diseases, such as California and Idaho.<br>· Use furrow irrigation.<br>· Improve airflow and avoid overhead sprayer irrigation.<br>· Rouge plants and rotate with non-legume crops. |
| Lettuce Mosaic Virus (LMV) (also affects escarole, endive, pea, and spinach) | Various pathogens | · Ensure seed hygiene.<br>· Manage aphids.<br>· Manage weeds. |
| Rust | *Uromyces* fungus | · Purchase resistant varieties.<br>· Use crop rotation.<br>· Avoid leaf-wetting.<br>· Reduce foliage wetness. |
| White Mold (Timber Rot, Drop, Stem Rot) | *Sclerotinia* fungus | · Destroy (burn) infected crops and weeds.<br>· Manage weeds. |
| Wilt | *Fusarium oxysporum* f. sp. *lycopersici* | · Ensure general hygiene.<br>· Ensure seed hygiene.<br>· Destroy infected crops (burn).<br>· Use crop rotation.<br>· Avoid excessive nitrogen.<br>· Manage soil acidity. |

# MINT/HERB FAMILY (*LAMIACEAE*)

The difference between the two EPA Groups, 19 and 25, is that Group 19: Herbs and Spices provide more than one consumer product. Some plants in Group 19 are consumed fresh and dried, while others provide leaves and seeds (cilantro [foliage] and coriander [seeds]). Interestingly, Group 19 includes celery seeds, although the plant is included in the group for non-brassica leafy vegetables (Group 4). The management regimen of herbs is similar to Group 4. Note that herbs are shallow rooted and need regular watering totaling 1 to 1½ inches (25 to 38 mm) per week.

In this photo, I'm in the process of planting up a stone raised bed with an array of new herbs. My dedication to cultivating a thriving herb garden is evident as I carefully arrange each plant to optimize growth and visual appeal.

| Common Name | Botanical Name | Management Approach (EPA) |
|---|---|---|
| Basil | *Ocimum basilicum* | Group 19: Herbs and Spices |
| Hyssop | *Hyssopus officinalis* | Group 19: Herbs and Spices |
| Lavender | *Lavandula* | Group 19: Herbs and Spices |
| Marjoram | *Origanum majorana* | Group 19: Herbs and Spices |
| Mint | *Mentha* | Group 25: Herbs |
| Oregano | *Origanum vulgare* | Group 19: Herbs and Spices |
| Perilla | *Perilla frutescens* | Group 25: Herbs |
| Rosemary | *Rosmarinus officinalis* | Group 25: Herbs |
| Sage | *Salvia officinalis* | Group 25: Herbs |
| Savory | *Satureja montana* | Group 19: Herbs and Spices |
| Thyme | *Thymus vulgaris* | Group 19: Herbs and Spices |

# MALLOW FAMILY (*MALVACEAE*)

### *Okra (Abelmoschus esculentus)*

Okra is a warm-season vegetable that can be grown in most regions with long summers. It produces edible pods that are rich in fiber, vitamin C, and antioxidants. To grow okra, prepare a sunny spot in your garden with well-drained soil with a pH of 6.0 to 6.8. Sow okra seeds directly in the ground after the last frost date or start them indoors four to six weeks before transplanting. Okra seeds must be soaked in water for twenty-four hours before planting to accelerate germination.

Okra plants need regular watering and fertilizing to thrive. Apply a balanced fertilizer every four to six weeks or use compost or manure as organic alternatives. You should also mulch around the plants to conserve moisture and suppress weeds. Okra plants can grow up to 6 feet (183 cm) tall, so you may need to stake them or use cages to support them.

Okra pods are ready to harvest when they are about 3 to 4 inches (8 to 10 cm) long, usually fifty to sixty days after planting. You should harvest okra pods every other day, or they will become tough and woody. Use a sharp knife or scissors to cut the pods from the stem, leaving a small portion of the stem attached. You should wear gloves when harvesting okra, as some varieties have spines that can irritate your skin.

Okra pods can be stored in the refrigerator for up to a week or frozen, canned, or dried for extended storage. Okra is a versatile vegetable that can be enjoyed in many dishes and cuisines.

Okra is a warm-season vegetable that requires a long summer.

| | | | |
|---|---|---|---|
| **Also Called:** | Love United, Ochro, Gumbo | **Root Health:** | Soil that offers good drainage and is rich in organic matter |
| **Difficulty:** | Medium | **Soil Temperature:** | 60°F to 70°F (15.5°C to 21°C) |
| **Ambient Temperature:** | Warm season | **Soil pH:** | 6.5 to 7.2 |
| **Hardiness Zones:** | 8 to 11 | **Tolerance:** | Can tolerate clay |
| **Life Cycle:** | Annual | **Emergence:** | Plant from cuttings |
| **Light:** | Full sun | **Airflow:** | 12 to 18 inches (30 to 45 cm) in-row and 36 to 48 inches (91 to 122 cm) between rows |
| **Height:** | 3 to 5 feet (91 to 152 cm) | **Spread:** | 3 to 5 feet (91 to 152 cm) |
| **Notes:** | Root rot can develop in waterlogged soil. Watch out for powdery mildew. Aphids, corn earworms, slugs, whiteflies, and spider mites are just a few of the insects that can cause problems. It is recommended to wear gloves when handling the plants as their hairs might cause irritation. The first fruit will be ready to harvest in fifty to sixty days. An individual fruit is ready to harvest four to six days after pollination. | | |

## Okra Fertilizer Recommendations

Okra should be given two equal amounts of nitrogen side-dressings: apply three to four weeks after planting and give a second application three to four weeks after the first. Phosphorus and potassium quantities for okra are slightly higher than other plants and should be added to the soil before planting. In the table below the imperial amounts are for a 40-square foot bed (10 × 4 ft) and the metric amounts are for a 3.6-meter bed (3 × 1.2 m).

[right] Okra pods are ready to pick when they are 3 to 4 inches (8 to 10 cm) long.

| Recommended NPK fertilizers | | | | | | | | |
|---|---|---|---|---|---|---|---|---|
| Crop | N Starter | | N Side-dressings | | Phosphorus (P) | | Potassium (K) | |
| Okra | 1.10 oz | 30.26 g | 0.44 oz | 12.11 g | 2.20 oz | 60.53 g | 2.20 oz | 60.53 g |

## Mitigating Okra Risks

### *Common Pests*

Aphids, caterpillars, Japanese beetles, mites, and stink bugs are common pests. Other pests that may affect okra crops include corn earworm, which damage leaves, buds, flowers and pods, and armyworms able to skeletonize leaves. It sounds worse than it is, as okra is generally pest resistant.

| Common Diseases | | |
|---|---|---|
| Disease | Pathogen | Prevention |
| Fusarium Wilt | *Fusarium* fugus | • Plant resistant cultivars.<br>• Use crop rotation—avoiding beds with a Fusarium basal rot history.<br>• Increase beneficial microbes by compost addition.<br>• Manage soil insects and foliar diseases.<br>• Avoid rotation with either the Cucurbitaceae or Solanaceae families. |
| Powdery Mildew | Cleistothecium from various fungi | • Select resistant cultivars.<br>• Rogue all plant debris at the end of the season.<br>• Avoid rotational planting with cucurbit plants. |

# BANANA FAMILY (*MUSACEAE*)

*Musa × paradisiaca* (the epithet means belonging to paradise) is a sterile hybrid of *M. acuminata × M. balbisiana*. While plantains can flourish in cooler regions, they only bear fruit in warmer climates or greenhouses. There are approximately a thousand banana varieties, of which a hundred are plantain varieties.

Plant cuttings about 12 to 24 inches (30 to 60 cm) deep at the beginning of the wet season. Plant spacing varies depending on the variety. Weeding should begin approximately six weeks after planting and be done regularly until the plants are tall enough to shade out rival plants. Plantain grows best in full sun, organically rich, medium moisture, well-drained soil. Ensure the roots have consistent access to moisture. Plantains are high feeders and need regular fertilization during the growing season. Plants should be placed in wind-protected areas to avoid damage to the huge leaves.

[right] Plantains are not typical home garden crops in temperate growing zones, but they are a staple food for many tropical regions of the world.

| Also Called: | Cooking Banana | Root Health: | Consistently moist, organically rich, medium moisture, well-drained soil |
|---|---|---|---|
| Difficulty: | High maintenance | Soil Temperature: | 98°F (37°C) |
| Ambient Temperature: | Tropics | Soil pH: | 5.5 to 7.0 |
| Hardiness Zones: | 9 to 11 | Tolerance: | Intolerant of frost but will reemerge |
| Life Cycle: | Herbaceous perennial | Emergence: | *Musa × paradisiaca* (*M. acuminata × M. balbisiana*) is a sterile triploid |
| Light: | Full sun–midday shade | Airflow: | Space well apart |
| Height: | 7 to 25 feet (2.1 to 7.6 m) | Spread: | 6 to 10 feet (1.8 to 3 m) |
| Notes: | Plantains are vegetatively propagated from shoots at the base of the plant (suckers) or from corms. | | |

# GRASS FAMILY (*POACEAE*)

| Common Name | Botanical Name | Management Approach (EPA) |
|---|---|---|
| Barley | *Hordeum vulgare* | Group 15: Cereal Grains |
| Corn | *Zea mays* | Group 15: Cereal Grains |
| Pearl Millet | *Pennisetum glaucum (Cenchrus americanus)* | Group 15: Cereal Grains |
| Oats | *Avena sativa* | Group 15: Cereal Grains |
| Rye | *Secale cereale* | Group 15: Cereal Grains |
| Wheat | *Triticum* | Group 15: Cereal Grains |

## Growing Corn

Plant the seeds about 1 inch (2.5 cm) deep and 4 inches (10 cm) apart in rows that are about 3 feet (91 cm) apart when soil temperatures are 77°F (25°C) and the danger of frost has passed. Plant them in blocks of four rows for better pollination. Corn is wind-pollinated, so you need to plant enough plants to ensure good kernel development. A minimum of ten to fifteen plants is recommended.

Water the plants regularly and deeply, especially during the flowering and ear development stages. Corn needs about 1 inch of water (25 mm) per week, but more in hot and dry weather. Mulch the soil to conserve moisture and prevent weeds.

Corn is a heavy feeder, so fertilize the plants with a balanced fertilizer (10–10–10) when they are about 1 foot (30 cm) tall and again when they start to tassel. Side-dress them with compost or manure every few weeks.

Harvest the ears when they are fully developed and the silk is brown and dry. Check the ripeness by peeling back the husk and piercing a kernel with your fingernail. If the juice is milky, the ear is ready. If it is clear, it is too early. If it is doughy, it is too late. Twist and pull the ears from the stalks and enjoy them fresh or store them for later use.

## Corn Fertilizer Recommendations

Maintain a soil pH between 6.2 and 6.8. Potassium is critical for healthy corn growth, and timely nitrogen side-dressings will boost foliage development in the growing season (spring). A four-yearly application of potash may be needed: 1.76 ounces per 10-foot bed (48 g per 3-m bed), but use soil-test results to inform all you nutrition decisions. In the table below the imperial amounts are for a 40-square foot bed (10 × 4 ft) and the metric amounts are for a 3.6-meter bed (3 × 1.2 m).

[top right] A vibrant patch of corn proudly stands in the Simplify Gardening garden, showcasing tall, healthy stalks and lush green leaves.

[bottom right] Corn earworm is a destructive pest of sweet corn in the home garden and on commercial farms.

| Recommended NPK fertilizers | | | | | | | | |
|---|---|---|---|---|---|---|---|---|
| Crop | N Starter | | N Side-dressings | | Phosphorus (P) | | Potassium (K) | |
| Sweet Corn | 0.73 oz | 20.18 g | 0.73 oz | 20.18 g | 1.76 oz | 48.42 g | 1.76 oz | 48.42 g |

## Mitigating Cereal Grain Risks

### Common Pests

Aphids, caterpillars, corn rootworm beetles and larvae, corn earworms, flea beetles, seed and root maggots, seed-corn beetles, slender corn beetles, stink bugs, and wireworms. Gardeners can minimize the impact of pests by ensuring their crops are healthy. Early stage plants are most susceptible, so protect your seedlings. Look for hybrids that provide rapid germination, early vigor, and other pest-resistant features.

| Common Diseases | | |
|---|---|---|
| Disease | Pathogen | Prevention |
| Anthracnose | *Colletotrichum graminicola* | • Plant resistant hybrids and varieties.<br>• Healthy, well-nourished plants are more resilient—ensure optimal soil fertility by planting multi-family cover crops.<br>• Rotate away from corn for a year or two. |
| Goss's Wilt | *Clavibacter michiganensis* ssp. *nebraskensis* bacterium | • Rotate to non-host crops for a year or two.<br>• Use disease-free seed and resistant varieties.<br>• Control grassy weeds that host the pathogen. |
| Northern Corn Leaf Blight (NCLB) | *Exserohilum turcicum* fungus | • Plant hybrids less susceptible to the disease.<br>• Use crop rotation.<br>• Practice good residue management. |
| Northern Corn Leaf Spot | *Bipolaris zeicola* | • Plant hybrids less susceptible to the disease.<br>• Use crop rotation.<br>• Practice good residue management. |
| Rust | *Puccinia* fungus | • Use resistant corn hybrids. |
| Smut | *Ustilago maydis* | • Infected plants should be removed and destroyed.<br>• Plant varieties of corn that have resistance to smut.<br>• Healthy plants are more resilient. Maintain recommended fertility levels in corn production.<br>• Avoid plant injury and insect damage. |
| Southern Corn Leaf Blight | *Cochliobolus heterostrophus* | • Use resistant hybrids.<br>• Use crop rotation. |
| Stewart's Wilt | *Pantoea (Erwinia) stewartii* bacterium | • Plant wilt-resistant, or partially resistant hybrids.<br>• Monitor overwintering flea beetle population. |
| Viruses | Several pathogens | • Plant resistant or partially resistant varieties.<br>• Avoid planting corn near small-grain crops.<br>• Manage aphids. |

# BUCKWHEAT/PETIOLE FAMILY (*POLYGONACEAE*)

### Rhubarb (Rheum rhabarbarum)

Rhubarb is a perennial vegetable that often is used in desserts, such as pies and crumbles, but it be used in savory dishes such as stews and sauces. The scientific name for rhubarb is *Rheum rhabarbarum*, and it belongs to the Polygonaceae family, which also includes buckwheat and sorrel.

Rhubarb is native to Asia but has been cultivated in Europe for hundreds of years. The plant has large, triangular-shaped leaves that can grow up to 2 feet (60 cm) long and a thick, fleshy stem or stalk that can range in color from green to red. The stem is the consumed part of the plant used in cooking, while the leaves are toxic and should not be eaten.

Rhubarb is a cool-season crop that can be grown in various climates, but it prefers well-drained soil and full sun. It is usually grown from crowns or root divisions and can take a few years to establish before it produces a harvestable crop. The stems are usually harvested in late spring or early summer and should be pulled rather than cut from the plant.

One of the unique features of rhubarb is its tart flavor due to the presence of oxalic acid. This can make it challenging to pair with other ingredients, but it can be balanced with sweeteners such as sugar or honey. Rhubarb also is a good source of vitamins C and K, fiber, and antioxidants.

Overall, rhubarb is a versatile and exciting plant that is beloved by many for its unique flavor and culinary applications.

You should only use young, healthy crowns with at least two buds. Plant 2 inches deep (5 cm) spaced three feet (91 cm) apart with rows that are 5 to 6 feet (152 to 183 cm) apart. Cut down flower stalks to encourage new root growth. Bolting can be triggered in plants of any age by several factors, including overexposure to light, soil deficiency, severe temperatures, and prolonged periods of drought. It takes between three and eight years to fully establish a planting and get it producing. Forcing involves putting crowns on an open dirt floor, or in apple crates, and piling a few inches of soil around them in a dark environment. Dormancy in plants is achieved at temperatures below 40°F (4.44°C).

[top] A magnificent rhubarb plant, boasting large, lush leaves and robust stalks is at home in the Simplify Gardening garden.

[bottom] Carefully select and harvest the best rhubarb stalks. With a keen eye for quality and an experienced touch, you can ensure only the finest produce makes its way from the garden to the kitchen.

## Rhubarb Fertilizer Recommendations

Maintain a soil pH between 6.0 and 6.5. Potassium is critical for healthy rhubarb growth, and timely nitrogen side-dressings will boost foliage development in the growing season (spring). A four-yearly application of potash may be needed: 1.76 ounces per 10-foot bed or (48.42 g per 3-m bed) but use soil-test results to inform all your nutrition decisions. In the table below the imperial amounts are for a 40-square foot bed (10 × 4 ft) and the metric amounts are for a 3.6-meter bed (3 × 1.2 m).

[right] These two enormous rhubarb stems make an impressive harvest. Despite their large size, these rhubarb stems remain sweet and tender, without any stringiness when eaten.

| Recommended NPK fertilizers | | | | | | | | | |
|---|---|---|---|---|---|---|---|---|---|
| Crop | N Starter | | N Side-dressings | | Phosphorus (P) | | Potassium (K) | |
| Rhubarb | 0.73 oz | 20.18 g | 0.73 oz | 20.18 g | 1.10 oz | 30.26 g | 1.91 oz | 52.46 g |

## Mitigating Rhubarb Risks

### *Common Pests*

Aphids, caterpillars, flea beetles, leafhoppers, curculio beetles, stink bugs, and whiteflies are all pests to watch out for. While rhubarb can be affected by these, the most common challenger is the garden slug, which can be controlled easily with good garden sanitation practices.

This healthy crown has two emerging leaves. The vibrant green leaves and the overall vigor of the crown mean you'll have strong, thriving plants.

| Common Diseases | | |
|---|---|---|
| Disease | Pathogen | Prevention |
| Gray Mold | *Botrytis cinerea* | • Ensure optimal airflow.<br>• Ensure good hygiene.<br>• Ensure good drainage. |
| Phytophthora Blight | *Phytophthora* oomycete | • Ensure seed hygiene.<br>• Use raised mounds (hills).<br>• Ensure good drainage. |

# NIGHTSHADE FAMILY (*SOLANACEAE*)

| Common Name | Botanical Name | Management Approach (EPA) |
| --- | --- | --- |
| Eggplant | *Solanum melongena* | Group 8: Fruiting Vegetables |
| Pepper (Sweet) | *Capsicum annuum* | Group 8: Fruiting Vegetables |
| Pepper (Chile) | *Capsicum annuum, C. chinense, C. frutescens* | Group 8: Fruiting Vegetables |
| Potato | *Solanum tuberosum* | Group 1: Root and Tuber Vegetables |
| Tomato | *Solanum lycopersicum* | Group 8: Fruiting Vegetables |

## Managing Fruiting Vegetables

### Eggplants (*Solanum melongena*)

Whether you prefer the dark 'Hansel' F1 hybrid, or the white 'Gretel', eggplants, also known as aubergine or brinjal, offer dramatic foliage and colorful fruits. The plant can be either an annual or a short-lived perennial and is highly susceptible to cold temperatures. It thrives in temperatures between 77°F and 85°F (25°C and 29°C), which is when it grows at its fastest rate. The fruit it produces is edible and has a high-gloss peel.

Eggplant plants grow 2 to 4 feet (61 to 122 cm) tall. Though it can be grown as an ornamental, eggplants are mainly grown for the nutritious fruit pulp filled with vitamins $B_1$, $B_6$, and C, nutritional fiber, and antioxidants. Eggplants offer a range of fruit shapes and colors, from long and thin types that resemble a shiny summer squash, or small, round types that look more like tomatoes. They are available in a wide array of hues, including white, green, pink, purple, brown, and striped. Fruits from ornamental eggplants resemble tiny pumpkins in color and shape and can even be dried.

For optimal growth, the eggplant thrives in full sunlight and prefers fertile, consistently moist, well-drained, and loamy soil in the pH range between 5.4 to 6.8. Propagation is done through seeds; germination typically takes eight

These small, nearly black-skinned eggplants are growing in the polytunnel. They are surrounded by lush green foliage, highlighting their vibrant growth in the controlled environment.

to fourteen days. The fruit is usually ready to be harvested within fifteen to eighteen weeks.

### Peppers (Capsicum annuum, C. chinense, C. frutescens, and C. pubescens)

Growing peppers is rewarding and fun, allowing you to produce various delicious and colorful fruits. Peppers belong to the genus *Capsicum*, which includes hot peppers such as jalapeños and habaneros and sweet peppers such as bell peppers and banana peppers. Peppers can be grown indoors or outdoors, depending on the climate and available space.

You will need some basic supplies to grow peppers, such as seeds or seedlings, pots or containers, potting soil, fertilizer, stakes or cages, and water. You also need a sunny location with at least six hours of direct sunlight daily. Peppers prefer warm temperatures, so avoid planting them too early or too late in the season. The ideal temperature range for peppers is between 70°F (21°C) and 85°F (29°C).

To start your peppers from seeds, you must sow them indoors about eight to ten weeks before the last frost date in your area. Fill small pots or trays with moist potting soil and place two or three seeds per pot. Cover the seeds lightly with soil and keep them warm until they germinate, which may take one to three weeks. Water the seedlings regularly and thin them to one plant per pot when they have two sets of true leaves.

To transplant your peppers outdoors, you must harden them off gradually by exposing them to outdoor conditions for a few hours each day for a week or two. Choose a sunny spot in your garden or patio with well-drained soil enriched with organic matter. Dig holes about 18 inches (45 cm) apart and set the plants, so the soil level is the same as in the pots. Water them well and apply a balanced fertilizer according to the package directions.

To care for your peppers, you will need to water them regularly, especially during hot and dry weather. Avoid overwatering or underwatering them, which can cause stress and affect their growth and fruit production. You also need to stake or cage your plants to support their stems and prevent them from breaking under the weight of the fruits. Prune your plants by pinching off the first few flowers to encourage more branching and fruiting.

To harvest your peppers, you must wait until they reach the desired size, color, and flavor. Peppers can be harvested at any stage of maturity, but they tend to be sweeter and more nutritious when fully ripe. Use scissors or a sharp knife to cut the peppers from the plants, leaving a short stem attached. Handle the peppers carefully and avoid touching your eyes or mouth after handling hot peppers. Store your peppers in the refrigerator for up to two weeks or preserve them by freezing, drying, pickling, or canning.

[top] A couple of large eggplants rest on the ground. These substantial fruits showcase the potential of well-tended plants to produce abundant and sizable harvests.

[bottom] Here, a seed tray is being prepared for sowing eggplant seeds. The tray is filled with nutrient-rich potting mix, providing the perfect environment for the seeds to germinate and grow into healthy seedlings.

[top left] A thriving chile pepper plant, loaded with numerous peppers, is growing inside the Simplify Gardening polytunnel.

[top right] The abundance of peppers hiding among the lush foliage of this pepper plant, combined with the vibrant green leaves are confirmation of a healthy plant.

[above] These impressive, large poblano peppers were grown as part of the Chili Grow Off with ChiliChump. The healthy, shiny peppers showcase the successful cultivation and care provided by the gardener.

[left] A long, deep red spaghetti chile stands out against the background. The rich color of the chile indicates its ripeness.

### *Tomatoes (Solanum lycopersicum)*

Tomatoes are not difficult to grow, but they do require some basic care and attention. Here are some tips on how to grow healthy and productive tomato plants:

- Choose a sunny and well-drained spot for your tomato plants. Tomatoes need at least six hours of direct sunlight daily to produce well. Avoid planting them in low-lying areas where water may accumulate and cause root rot.

- Prepare the soil before planting. Tomatoes prefer rich and loamy soil with a pH of 6.0 to 6.8. You can improve your soil by adding organic matter such as compost, manure, or peat moss. Add some fertilizer or lime to adjust the pH and nutrient levels according to a soil test.

- Plant your tomato seedlings after the last frost date in your area. Start your own seedlings indoors about six to eight weeks before planting or buy them from a nursery or garden center. Dig a hole deep enough to cover the stem to the first set of leaves when planting. This will help the plant develop a robust root system. Space your plants about 18 to 24 inches (45 to 60 cm) apart in rows that are 3 to 4 feet (91 cm to 1.2 m) apart.

- Support your tomato plants with stakes, cages, or trellises. This will keep the plants upright and prevent them from sprawling on the ground, where they may be exposed to pests, diseases, and rotting. Tie the stems loosely to the supports with twine or clips as they grow.

- Water your tomato plants regularly and deeply. Tomatoes need about 1 inch (2.5 cm) of water weekly (more in hot and dry weather). Water the soil around the base of the plants, not the leaves, to avoid fungal diseases. Use a soaker hose or a drip irrigation system to deliver water efficiently and evenly.

- Mulch your tomato plants with straw, grass clippings, leaves, or plastic. Mulching will help conserve soil moisture, suppress weeds, and moderate soil temperature. It also prevents soilborne diseases from splashing onto the leaves and fruits.

- Prune your tomato plants if needed. Pruning is optional, but it can help improve air circulation, reduce disease problems, and increase fruit size and quality. Prune your plants by removing the suckers, which are the small shoots that grow between the main stem and the branches. Remove some of the lower leaves that may touch the ground or shade the fruits.

- Harvest your tomatoes when they are ripe and ready. Tomatoes are ripe when they have reached their full color and are slightly soft to the touch. Pick them off the vine by twisting them gently or using a pair of scissors or a knife. Enjoy your fresh tomatoes or store them in a cool, dark place for up to a week.

[top] This is a rare tomato megabloom, which is a cluster of flowers on one stem, vital for growing giant tomatoes.

[bottom] A beautiful truss of cherry tomatoes growing in my polytunnel.

## Fertilizer Recommendations for Fruiting Vegetables and Potatoes

Maintain a soil pH between 6.0 and 6.5 for all the fruiting vegetables, but you need a slightly more acidic soil for potatoes (5.8 to 6.2). The Solanaceae family are all sensitive to chlorine, though eggplants less so. Potassium is critical for healthy fruit growth, and timely nitrogen side-dressings will boost development in the growing season (spring). Tomatoes will benefit from a boron application—0.02 ounces per 40-square foot bed or 0.61 grams per 3.6-square meter bed. Make a batch that includes a bulking agent to help get a lower concentration for easier spreading. Generally, boron applications are a pound or two per acre and the above calculations are based on 1.5 pounds (680 g) per acre. Most vegetable crops benefit from a boron application (same ratio), excluding the Fabaceae, Cucurbitaceae, and Asteraceae families. Also don't add it to herb and spinach crops.

In the table below the imperial amounts are for a 40-square foot bed (10 × 4 ft) and the metric amounts are for a 3.6-meter bed (3 × 1.2 m).

| Recommended NPK fertilizers | | | | | | | | |
|---|---|---|---|---|---|---|---|---|
| Crop | N Starter | | N Side-dressings | | Phosphorus (P) | | Potassium (K) | |
| Eggplants | 1.10 oz | 30.26 g | 0.51 oz | 14.12 g | 2.20 oz | 60.53 g | 2.20 oz | 60.53 g |
| Peppers | 0.73 oz | 20.18 g | 0.40 oz | 10.89 g | 2.20 oz | 60.53 g | 2.20 oz | 60.53 g |
| Potatoes | 1.47 oz | 40.35 g | 0 oz | 0 g | 1.32 oz | 36.32 g | 2.20 oz | 60.53 g |
| Tomatoes | 0.59 oz | 16.14 g | 0.59 oz | 16.14 g | 2.20 oz | 60.53 g | 2.94 oz | 80.70 g |

## Mitigating Fruiting Vegetable Risks

### *Physiological Disorders*

**Blossom End Rot:** Avoid irrigation fluctuations and excessive ammonia-based fertilizer

**Catfacing:** Watch for very low temperatures during blossoming, or get variety resistant to the deformity.

**Cracks:** Manage irrigation consistency, especially in hot weather. Keep an adequate balance between fruit and foliage—can be caused by too little foliage from pruning.[82]

**Sunscald:** Same as above—ensure adequate foliage.

Blossom end rot is an unfortunate disorder of tomatoes when they are not watered consistently.

## *Common Pests*

Some common pests that can affect fruiting vegetable plants include aphids, whiteflies, mites, armyworms, loopers, tobacco hornworms, tomato hornworms, cabbage maggots, carrot rust flies, corn earworms, tomato fruitworms, cowpea curculios, and stink bugs.

| Common Diseases | | |
|---|---|---|
| **Disease** | **Pathogen** | **Prevention** |
| Anthracnose | *Colletotrichum* fungus | • Use disease-free seed and transplants.<br>• Ensure seed hygiene.<br>• Rotate to non-Solanaceous crops for three to four years.<br>• Ensure proper drainage, soil temperatures, and airflow.<br>• Reduce splashing.<br>• Promptly rogue finished crops. |
| Bacterial Canker | *Clavibacter* bacteria | • Use crop rotation.<br>• Choose seeds and seedlings from a reputable supplier.<br>• Avoid wetting leaves.<br>• Ensure adequate airflow.<br>• Rogue plants at the end of the season. |
| Bacterial Speck | *Pseudomonas syringae* | • Ensure general hygiene.<br>• Avoid working with wet plants.<br>• Keep foliage dry. |
| Bacterial Spot | *Xanthomonas* bacteria | • Plant pathogen-free seed or transplants.<br>• Ensure seed hygiene.<br>• Keep leaves dry.<br>• Don't work with wet plants.<br>• Practice general tool hygiene. |
| Tomato Buckeye Rot | *Phytophthora* oomycete | • Ensure proper drainage.<br>• Plant in raised beds.<br>• Rotate to non-Solanaceous crops.<br>• Stake and/or mulch plants to reduce contact with soil. |
| Damping-off Seed and Seedling Rots | Various pathogens, including *Fusarium* spp. and *Pythium* spp. | • Ensure general hygiene.<br>• Use warmer water, 68°F to 77°F (20°C to 25°C).<br>• Improve drainage. |
| Early Blight | *Alternaria* fungus | • Plant tolerant varieties.<br>• Maintain plant vigor.<br>• Remove volunteer weeds.<br>• Rotate to non-Solanaceous crops for three to four years. |
| Fusarium Wilt | *Fusarium* fungus | • Plant resistant varieties.<br>• Rotate to non-Solanaceous crops for three to four years.<br>• Use raised beds, replacing soil if needed. |

| Common Diseases | | |
| --- | --- | --- |
| Disease | Pathogen | Prevention |
| Gray Mold | *Botrytis* fungus | • Ensure airflow.<br>• Practice good plant hygiene.<br>• Work only with dry plants.<br>• Maintain adequate consistent soil moisture. |
| Late Blight | *Phytophthora* oomycete | • Where possible, plant resistant varieties.<br>• Plant early in the season to escape high disease pressure later in the season.<br>• Keep foliage dry.<br>• Scout plants often, removing infected plants, fruit, volunteers, and weeds. |
| Leaf Blight | *Septoria* fungus | • Start with certified disease-free seed.<br>• Improve air circulation.<br>• Keep foliage dry.<br>• Don't work with wet plants.<br>• Destroy infected plants (burn). |
| Leaf Mold | *Passalora* fungus | • Avoid getting foliage wet; use drip irrigation.<br>• Improve air movement between rows and individual plants. Lift plants.<br>• General tool and stake hygiene: sterilize with alcohol or 10 percent bleach solution.<br>• Remove crop residue at the end of the season. Burn it or bury it away from tomato production areas. |
| Nematodes | Nematodes | • Increase soil compost content to boost beneficial microorganism populations.<br>• Consider anaerobic soil disinfection (ASD), a form of soil solarization. |
| Phytophthora Blight | *Phytophthora infestans* | • Same as leaf blight. |
| Powdery Mildew | *Leveillula* fungus | • Avoid fields with a history of the disease.<br>• Rotate to non-Solanaceous crops for two years.<br>• Improve airflow by using stakes.<br>• Avoid wet foliage.<br>• Promptly destroy finished crops. |
| Southern Blight | *Sclerotium* fungus | • Same as for powdery mildew. |
| Viruses | Several pathogens | • Manage aphid populations as they spread viruses.<br>• Ensure seed health.<br>• Ensure seed hygiene. |
| White Mold (Timber Rot, Drop, Stem Rot) | *Sclerotinia* fungus | • Destroy (burn) infected crops and weeds.<br>• Manage weeds. |
| Wilt | *Verticillium* fungus | • Select resistant varieties.<br>• Rotate to non-Solanaceous crops for two to three years.<br>• Consider soil solarization.<br>• Destroy infected plants.<br>• Sanitize tools and equipment.<br>• Consider earlier crops to alleviate heat pressures.<br>• Use mulch from resistant trees.<br>• Control weeds. |

# **Conclusion**

Our natural world's sustainability depends on prioritizing *its* well-being, ensuring we know what sustainable, simplified gardening is, and practicing it. The combined efforts of home gardeners can have significant environmental advantages and are easy to implement—but this requires a paradigm shift.

We, including me, must move from ownership to stewardship, from maximizing productivity at any cost to working collaboratively with Nature. Productivity and sustainability are not mutually exclusive; our gardening excellence is what the world needs.

This book provides an overview of the context in which we live, the environmental challenges we face, and how we, as home gardeners, can make a marked difference. As the world is forced to pursue more sustainable habits, including what we eat, vegetables will increasingly become the mainstay of most diets. I wrote the book to help gardeners worldwide better grow their own food, establishing local food sources for greater community resilience. While the need for this may not yet be a priority, I expect knowing how to care for food-producing plants will become an increasingly essential skill.

The first chapter addresses the elephant in the room, the topic we prefer to skirt. Our environment needs remedial action, action, I believe, best performed by those that love Nature's processes. Gardeners. Home gardeners command great swaths of land. In the United States, the surface area devoted to lawns alone is around 40 million acres (16.18 million ha), growing at a million acres (404,686 ha) annually. That's a lot of potential growing space to address the growing food insecurities many communities suffer.

The chapter also addresses our growing need for healthy food at scale. A growing population and extreme food-related public health challenges mean we will need to adapt, a change that necessitates moving to eat more vegetables. We explore food systems globally, drilling down to local community gardens and your garden. Part of this move, I believe, is needed to protect vulnerable people in local communities. The less a community needs to rely on external food systems, the more resilient their food supplies will be. Local food systems also boost local economies, keeping and growing local wealth.

Rather than focusing on how deep and far apart plants should be planted, the pH levels and nutrients individual plants need, or similar details, this book focuses on the principles behind growing any plant, specifically vegetables. Starting with the ecosystemic context, we drill down to plant environmental needs before we explore the needs (and risks) of sixteen vegetable families representing more than eighty vegetables and herbs.

To this end, the second chapter covers the ecosystemic context, the third chapter addresses the ten plant growth factors, followed by a look at how to optimize plant health, or minimally, how to minimize the risks. The final chapter explores the different plant families, their management needs, and how to defend them against pests and diseases.

Understanding how systems function, their interrelation, and how changing any individual part impacts the whole helps us make more informed decisions, improving our ability to act responsibly and collaboratively with Nature. On a micro-level, knowing the universal needs of plants, both above and below ground, helps us better care for them, ensuring their needs are met as they meet ours.

Plants are botanically grouped into families based on their reproductive characteristics, environmental needs, and shared risks. Plants also can be grouped by their cold hardiness or their management strategies. To make it easier for gardeners to manage their vegetable crops, I have grouped plants by management strategies with individual nutritional needs and shared pests and diseases (with their respective control methods).

An example is the shared needs of fruiting vegetables (e.g., tomatoes, peppers, eggplants/aubergines, and okra). While the first three are in the Solanaceae family with potatoes, their cousin is grouped with tuber and root crops, with carrots sharing common risks. The nutritional needs of the carrot are reflected in a table that includes its relatives in the Apiaceae family. The final chapter, therefore, is best read as a whole, allowing the reader to see the interrelationships across management and family groups.

# References

1. Willet, Walter, Johan Rockström, et al. 2019. *Summary Report of the EAT-Lancet Commission.* https://eatforum.org/content/uploads/2019/07/EAT-Lancet_Commission_Summary_Report.pdf.

2. Food and Agriculture Organization of the United Nations. 2023. "Home." www.fao.org/home/en.

3. Zereyesus, Yacob Abrehe, Lila Cardell, et al. 2022. "International Food Security Assessment, 2022-32." *USDA Economic Research Service.* Food Security Assessment Situation and Outlook No. (GFA-33) www.ers.usda.gov/webdocs/outlooks/104708/gfa-33_summary.pdf.

4. Hunger in America. (n.d.). Feedingamerica.org. www.feedingamerica.org/hunger-in-america.

5. Barrett, Christopher, Emily Broad Leib, et al. 2021. "True Cost of Food: Measuring What Matters to Transform the U.S. Food System." The Rockefeller Foundation. www.rockefellerfoundation.org/report/true-cost-of-food-measuring-what-matters-to-transform-the-u-s-food-system.

6. Marsden, T., & Morley, A. (Eds.). (2014). *Sustainable food systems: Building a new paradigm.* Routledge. www.fao.org/3/ca2079en/CA2079EN.pdf.

7. Stockholm Resilience Centre, Stockholm University. 2022. "Planetary Boundaries." www.stockholmresilience.org/research/planetary-boundaries.html.

8. Willet, Walter, Johan Rockström, et al. 2019. *Summary Report of the EAT-Lancet Commission.* https://eatforum.org/content/uploads/2019/07/EAT-Lancet_Commission_Summary_Report.pdf.

9. United States Senate Committee on Agriculture, Nutrition, & Forestry. 2021. "The State of Nutrition in America 2021." Filmed November 2021 at 216 Hart Senate Office Building, Washington, D.C. Video. www.agriculture.senate.gov/hearings/the-state-of-nutrition-in-america-2021.

10. Mozaffarian, Dariush. 2021. "The State of Nutrition in America 2021." United States Senate Committee on Agriculture, Nutrition, & Forestry. November 2, 2021. www.agriculture.senate.gov/imo/media/doc/Testimony_Mozaffarian_11.02.2021_UPDATED1.pdf.

11. Jaglo, Kirsten, S. Kenny, and J. Stephenson. 2021. "Part 1: From Farm to Kitchen: The Environmental Impacts of U.S. Food Waste." *U.S. Environmental Protection Agency Office of Research and Development.* (EPA 600-R21 171) www.epa.gov/system/files/documents/2021-11/from-farm-to-kitchen-the-environmental-impacts-of-u.s.-food-waste_508-tagged.pdf.

12. Kelloway, Claire and Sarah Miller. 2019. "Report | Food and Power: Addressing Monopolization in America's Food System." *Open Markets Institute.* www.openmarketsinstitute.org/publications/food-power-addressing-monopolization-americas-food-system.

13. Coley, David & Howard, Mark & Winter, Michael. (2011). Food miles: Time for a re-think?. *British Food Journal*. 113. 919-934. www.researchgate.net/publication/235272001_Food_miles_Time_for_a_re-think.

14. RE:TV. (2021, January 20). Little Leaf Farms. RE:TV. www.re-tv.org/articles/reworking-food-production.

15. United States Department of Agriculture, Rural Development. 2023. "Cooperative Services." www.rd.usda. gov/programs-services/all-programs/cooperative-services.

16. United States Department of Agriculture, Rural Business-Cooperative Service. 2017. *Federal Statutes of Special Importance to Farmer Cooperatives: 115th Congress Edition*. www.rd.usda.gov/sites/default/files/publications/ CIR66_CooperativeFederalStatutes.pdf.

17. United States Department of Agriculture, Rural Development. 2023. "Value-Added Producer Grants." www.rd.usda.gov/programs-services/business-programs/value-added-producer-grants.

18. 2021 National Gardening Survey. National Gardening Association. 2021. Gardenresearch.com. gardenresearch. com/view/national-gardening-survey-2021-edition.

19. Athearn, Kevin, Hannah Wooten, et al. 2021. "Costs and Benefits of Vegetable Gardening."https:// gardeningsolutions.ifas.ufl.edu/plants/edibles/vegetables/paper-vegetable-gardening-cost-analysis.html.

20. World Bank Group. 2023. *What is Food Security*. World Bank Group.

21. United States Department of Agriculture, National Institute of Food and Agriculture (NIFA). *Steps for a Hunger-Free Community*. www.nifa.usda.gov/sites/default/files/resources/Goals_for_ aHungerFreeCommunity.pdf

22. Stewart, H., & Hyman, J. *Price Spreads from Farm to Consumer*. United States Department of Agriculture. www. ers.usda.gov/data-products/price-spreads-from-farm-to-consumer.

23. United States Department of Agriculture, Office of Urban Agriculture and Innovative Production (OUAIP). www.usda.gov/urban.

24. LoRa Alliance. 2023. "LoRaWAN® Coverage." https://lora-alliance.org/lorawan-coverage.

25. MQ Telemetry Transport. www.mqtt.org.

26. *tinyML Talks: Creating Individualized Solutions for Industrial-Grade and Environmental Problems with TinyML*. Tinyml.org. www.tinyml.org/event/tinyml-talks-creating-individualized-solutions-for-industrial-grade-and-environmental-problems-with-tinyml.

27. Data visualization. (n.d.). ThingsBoard. thingsboard.io/docs/user-guide/visualization.

28. Balena.Io. www.balena.io/open.

29. Grafana Labs. grafana.com/docs/grafana/latest/fundamentals.

30. Maturana, Humberto R. and Francisco J. Varela. 1991. *Autopoiesis and Cognition: The Realization of the Living.* Boston: D. Reidel Publishing Company. Google Books. https://books.google.co.za/books?id=nVmcN9Ja68kC.

31. Centers for Disease Control and Prevention. 2021. "Adverse Childhood Experiences (ACEs)" www.cdc.gov/vitalsigns/aces/index.html.

32. Water Science School. 2018. "Groundwater Storage and the Water Cycle." www.usgs.gov/special-topics/water-science-school/science/groundwater-storage-and-water-cycle.

33. The University of Arizona. "Biosphere 2." https://biosphere2.org.

34. Biology Online. "Dominant Species." www.biologyonline.com/dictionary/dominant-species.

35. Resilience Alliance. 2015. "Adaptive Cycle." www.resalliance.org/adaptive-cycle.

36. Olson, David. 2011. "FACES IV and the Circumplex Model: Validation Study." *Journal of Marital and Family Therapy* 37, no. 1: 64–80.

37. Hickel, Jason. 2018. "The Nobel Prize for Climate Catastrophe." *Foreign Policy* 6. https://foreignpolicy.com/2018/12/06/the-nobel-prize-for-climate-catastrophe.

38. Hestrin, Rachel, Megan Kan, et al. 2022. "Plant-associated Fungi Support Bacterial Resilience following Water Limitation." *The ISME Journal* 16, no. 12: 2752–62. https://pubmed.ncbi.nlm.nih.gov/36085516.

39. Real Science. 2021. "The Secret Language of Trees." YouTube Video, 15:58. www.youtube.com/watch?v=9HiADisBfQ0.

40. Sustainable Agriculture Research and Education (SARE) Outreach. 2023. "Legume Cover Crops." www.sare.org/publications/managing-cover-crops-profitably/legume-cover-crops,

41. O'Neill, Tony. 2022. "What Are the Best Plants for Hydroponics?" Simplify Gardening. October 12, 2022. https://simplifygardening.com/best-plants-for-hydroponics.

42. Rosenthal, Ed and Anthony Petramala. 2019. *Growing Veggie.* 35th Space Symposium, Technical Track, Colorado Springs, Colorado, United States of America presented on April 8, 2019. www.spacefoundation.org/wp-content/uploads/2019/07/Paper-Rosenthal-Ed-InnovationsFromSpaceToEarth-Growing-Veggie.pdf.

43. Bainbridge, David A. 2012. "Overstory #249: Wick Irrigation for Tree Establishment." www.agroforestry.org/the-overstory/7-overstory-249-wick-irrigation-for-tree-establishment.

44. Project LAMP. Hortlamp.org.

45. Sheng-li, L. I., X. I. A. Ya-zhen, L. I. U. Jin, S. H. I. Xiao-dan, and S. U. N. Zhi-qiang. "Effects of cold-shock on tomato seedlings under high temperature stress." *Yingyong Shengtai Xuebao* 25, no. 10 (2014).

46. O'Neill, Tony. 2022. "Best Beautiful Succulents for Humid Rooms in Your Home." Simplify Gardening. October 26, 2022. https://simplifygardening.com/succulents-for-humid-rooms.

47. ———. 2022. "What Type of Humidifier Is Best for Plants?" Simplify Gardening. October 17, 2022. https://simplifygardening.com/humidifier-best-for-plants.

48. ———. 2022. "What Type of Humidifier Is Best for Plants?" Simplify Gardening. October 17, 2022. https://simplifygardening.com/humidifier-best-for-plants.

49. NASA. 2023. "Vital Signs of the Planet." https://climate.nasa.gov/vital-signs/carbon-dioxide.

50. O'Neill, Tony. 2022. "Why Is My Monstera Drooping?" Simplify Gardening. September 30, 2022. https://simplifygardening.com/why-is-my-monstera-drooping.

51. NASA. 1989. "Interior Landscape Plants for Indoor Air Pollution Abatement." https://ntrs.nasa.gov/api/citations/19930073077/downloads/19930073077.pdf.

52. NASA. 2023. "NASA Plant Research Offers a Breath of Fresh Air." https://spinoff.nasa.gov/Spinoff2019/cg_7 html.

53. O'Neill, Tony. 2022. "The Ultimate Guide to Monstera Leaves Turning Yellow." Simplify Gardening. October 6, 2022. https://simplifygardening.com/9-reasons-monstera-leaves-turn-yellow-prevent-and-fix.

54. ———. 2022. "The Ultimate Guide to Monstera Leaves Turning Yellow." Simplify Gardening. October 6, 2022. https://simplifygardening.com/9-reasons-monstera-leaves-turn-yellow-prevent-and-fix.

55. German Jena Experiment. "Main Experiment." https://the-jena-experiment.de/index.php/main-experiment.

56. Luo, Guangjuan. 2017. "Jena Experiment Intro English." Youtube. February 13, 2017. www.youtube.com/watch?v=j3SvG2nBCTM.

57. Food and Agriculture Organization (FAO) of the United Nations. "World Fertilizer Trends and Outlook to 2020." 2017. www.fao.org/3/i6895e/i6895e.pdf.

58. Stevens, P. F. 2001. *Angiosperm Phylogeny Website, version 14.* www.mobot.org/MOBOT/research/APweb.

59. Colorado State University. 2013. "Cultivars and Advanced Selections Home." https://potatoes.colostate.edu/our-team/about-us/programs/potato-breeding/cultivars.

60. Soil Science Division Staff. 2017. *Soil Survey Manual.* https://www.nrcs.usda.gov/sites/default/files/2022-09/The-Soil-Survey-Manual.pdf

61. Cornell University, Department of Plant Pathology, www.vegetables.cornell.edu/pest-management/disease-factsheets/cropping-sequences-and-root-health.

62. Armstrong McKay, David I., Arie Staal, et al. 2022. "Exceeding 1.5°C Global Warming Could Trigger Multiple Climate Tipping Points." *Science* 377, no. 6611. www.science.org/doi/10.1126/science.abn7950.

63. United States Environmental Protection Agency. 2023. "Sources of Greenhouse Gas Emissions." www.epa.gov/ghgemissions/sources-greenhouse-gas-emissions.

64. O'Neill, Tony. 2022. "What Are the Best Plants for Carbon Capture?" Simplify Gardening. October 17, 2022. https://simplifygardening.com/best-plants-for-carbon-capture.

65. Global Soil Biodiversity Initiative. 2023. "SoilBON." www.globalsoilbiodiversity.org/soilbon.

66. U.S. Climate Resilience Toolkit. 2021. "Ranchers in Marin County Consider Carbon Credits." https://toolkit.climate.gov/case-studies/ranchers-marin-county-consider-carbon-credits.

67. O'Neill, Tony. 2022. "What Are the Best Plants for Carbon Capture?" Simplify Gardening. October 17, 2022. https://simplifygardening.com/best-plants-for-carbon-capture.

68. ———. 2022. "Unlock the Full Potential of Composting with Nitrogen." Simplify Gardening. December 26, 2022. https://simplifygardening.com/you-wont-believe-the-shocking-benefits-of-nitrogen-in-compost.

69. ———. 2020. "Is Clay Soil Good for Plant Growth? The Facts." Simplify Gardening. January 27, 2020. https://simplifygardening.com/clay-soil-good.

70. ———. 2022. "The Best Bonsai Soil Mix for Bonsai Health." Simplify Gardening. July 19, 2022. https://simplifygardening.com/best-bonsai-soil-mix.

71. ———. 2022. "Unlock the Full Potential of Composting with Nitrogen." Simplify Gardening. December 26, 2022. https://simplifygardening.com/you-wont-believe-the-shocking-benefits-of-nitrogen-in-compost.

72. ———. 2021. "Aerobic Composting – Creating an Active Compost for Life." Simplify Gardening. November 10, 2021. https://simplifygardening.com/aerobic-composting-creating-an-active-soil-food-web.

73. ———. 2022. "Unlock the Full Potential of Composting with Nitrogen." Simplify Gardening. December 26, 2022. https://simplifygardening.com/you-wont-believe-the-shocking-benefits-of-nitrogen-in-compost.

74. ———. 2021. "Aerobic Composting – Creating an Active Compost for Life." Simplify Gardening. November 10, 2021. https://simplifygardening.com/aerobic-composting-creating-an-active-soil-food-web.

75. ———. 2022. "How Long Does It Take to Make Compost." Simplify Gardening. September 15, 2022. https://simplifygardening.com/how-long-does-it-take-to-make-compost.

76. ———. 2022. "How to Compost in a Tumbler." Simplify Gardening. September 15, 2022. https://simplifygardening.com/how-to-compost-in-a-tumbler.

77. ———. 2022. "Unlock the Full Potential of Composting with Nitrogen." Simplify Gardening. December 26, 2022. https://simplifygardening.com/you-wont-believe-the-shocking-benefits-of-nitrogen-in-compost.

78. Code of Federal Regulations. 2023. "Crop Group Tables." https://www.ecfr.gov/current/title-40/chapter-I/subchapter-E/part-180/subpart-B/section-180.41.

79. O'Neill, Tony. 2023. "The Ultimate Guide to Growing Carrots in Your Backyard." Simplify Gardening. January 12, 2023. https://simplifygardening.com/growing-carrots-in-your-backyard.

80. Testen, Anna L. and Sally A. Miller. 2017. "Anaerobic Soil Disinfestation." The Ohio State University. https://u.osu.edu/vegetablediseasefacts/management/anaerobic-soil-disinfestation. Anaerobic soil disinfestation or ASD is a method to reduce plant pathogens, weeds, and nematodes in the soil.

81. Vegetable Growers News. 2023. https://vegetablegrowersnews.com.

82. O'Neill, Tony. 2023. "Common Pepper Diseases and How to Prevent Them." Simplify Gardening. January 12, 2023. https://simplifygardening.com/common-pepper-diseases.

# About the Author

Tony O'Neill is a full-time firefighter and passionate gardener who loves Nature and helping others become great gardeners. His grandfather, a passionate gardener, instilled in him an early love of gardening. Tony attended a horticulture college in his childhood, which gave him a solid basis, but he maintains that Nature is the finest teacher. Of special interest to him as a global gardening influencer who has met thousands of gardeners is that, while the general principles apply, each garden has unique soil and climate conditions, requiring constant adaptation.

Sharing his love and learning started fourteen years ago when he initially launched his YouTube channel, Simplify Gardening, as a hobby. The channel has grown, and today Tony has more than a million followers across his network learning about gardening.

In 2021 Tony was awarded the Ezoic Publisher of the Year Award for Educational Content on YouTube and this website. Simplify Gardening is about helping gardeners succeed, whether you're a food gardener, house plant lover, bonsai grower, or succulent enthusiast. With his books and videos, Tony's goal is to make gardening simple, easy, and enjoyable for everyone, and help people grow their food and self-sufficiency.

"For the past four decades, I have dedicated myself to the study and practice of gardening, accumulating a wealth of knowledge and experience."

The Simplify Gardening website, YouTube channel, and other social media platforms allow Tony to share his discoveries and insights with the gardening community. These platforms give gardening enthusiasts easy access to years of research and experimentation and a wealth of information on various gardening topics.

Website: simplifygardening.com

YouTube Channel: youtube.com/simplifygardening

Facebook Page: facebook.com/simplifygardening

Facebook Group: www.facebook.com/groups/929703783720749

Instagram: www.instagram.com/simplifygardening

Twitter: twitter.com/simplifygarden

LinkedIn: www.linkedin.com/in/tukherewegrow

TikTok: www.tiktok.com/@simplifygardening

Patreon Page: www.patreon.com/simplifygardening

Odysee Channel: odysee.com/@simplifygardening:0

# Index